FROM KATA TO COMPETITION

The Complete Karate Handbook

Alex Sternberg
and Gary Goldstein

ARCO PUBLISHING, INC.
NEW YORK

Dedication

I respectfully dedicate this book to my wife Shelley and son Dov. Their understanding and support for my work over the years have sustained me.   A. S.

For my parents and sister, who never lost their faith in my future.   G. G.

Published by Arco Publishing, Inc.
219 Park Avenue South, New York, N.Y. 10003

Copyright © 1982 by Alex Sternberg and Gary Goldstein

Library of Congress Cataloging in Publication Data

Sternberg, Alex.
    From kata to competition.

    Includes index.
    1. Karate.   I. Goldstein, Gary.   II. Title.
GV1114.3.S86   796.8'153   81-15040
ISBN 0-668-05241-4 (Cloth edition)   AACR2
ISBN 0-668-05422-0 (Paper edition)

Printed in the United States of America

Contents

Authors' Note

The "I" in this book is the voice of Alex Sternberg—teacher, coach, judge, and former Nationals Champion. He started competing nationally in the late '60s and won such events as the All-American and the U.S., Canadian, and South American Nationals. He later joined the Amateur Athletic Union to coach U.S. National Teams for competition in Mexico, Venezuela, France, and Israel. He also opened up two shotokan dojos in New York, attained the rank of fourth-degree black belt, and organized the effort to introduce karate into the Macabiah Games starting in 1977.

Mr. Sternberg referees at national and international tournaments, is a member of the National Karate Board of the AAU, and is a delegate to the World Union of Karate Organizations. He presently promotes the annual Playboy Karate Classic at Great Gorge, New Jersey, and is working through the AAU to get karate included in the Olympic Games.

His coauthor, Gary Goldstein, is a writer and martial arts devotee who has written numerous articles about karate for *Black Belt* and *Official Karate* magazines and for the *International Encyclopedia of the Martial Arts*.

Acknowledgments

I began my karate training in the Williamsburg Y.M.H.A. with R. Chun, a Korean instructor. But it was only after I was accepted into Sensei George Cofield's Tong Dojo that I realized the full impact of a good teacher. I learned a great deal from both Sensei Cofield and Sensei Tom LaPuppet and when I began to teach, it was their method that I taught.

Over the years, as I gained experience, I began to modify and upgrade that method to reflect in my dojo the changes that were developing in karate. I received help in this from my students who have become respected instructors in their own right. Kenneth Inglima, Howard Frydman, Leah and Buckie Sukenik, Steve Eliach, and Roni Kopels did much to help prepare this book and I would like to express my gratitude for their contributions. Special thanks to Alan Zenreich for his excellent photography and to Yossi Schorr and Seth Boone for appearing in the photographs.

Alex Sternberg

Foreword

The history of karate has always been devoid of information concerning the roots and finer points of karate achievement. Many East Coast martial artists, for example, suffered from the formation of selective media exposure and the mainstream of karate growth was overshadowed by personality articles on strangers from foreign places—lending no support to the struggle of the American senseis and their students who paved the way for and supported this same media.

Times have not changed! However, Alex Sternberg, a pillar in the karate community and a true pioneer in the martial arts for thousands of karateka, has penetrated the karate archives to bring to light the various areas of self-defense and history few of us remember but should be aware of.

If it is true that opposites attract, then let Mr. Sternberg be a shining example of that. As a young man of fifteen, he stepped through the doors of the mighty Tong Dojo wearing his yarmulke and horn-rimmed glasses. Surrounded by hard-core survivors of the streets of the Brownsville ghetto in Brooklyn, he was challenged to test his karate at the Tong by Sensei George Cofield, did so, and has survived the changing tide of time to engrave his name in history by publishing his knowledgeable book on American karate as seen from the eyes of a shotokan master.

Thomas LaPuppet/fifth-degree black belt
Chairman, Metropolitan AAU
Black Belt Hall of Fame, 1969

Preface

Most karate textbooks divide their blocks, punches, kicks, and stances into separate chapters so that you can quickly find the particular technique you are interested in mastering. But because the individual who buys a textbook is usually a student and not a master, he won't know which kick to learn first, which block to learn first, and which punch to learn first. He not only doesn't know in what order to learn the techniques but, equally important, he's ignorant of how he should train his body. Consequently, he finds it difficult to correctly execute the techniques because his body isn't being properly trained.

To correct this problem, all the techniques in this book have been arranged into chapters based on their level of difficulty. In each chapter you'll find a certain number of blocking techniques, a certain number of hand techniques, and a certain number of kicking techniques. If you want to master all the techniques here, you must follow the order in which they are set down.

Since I began teaching fifteen years ago, I have experimented with a number of different programs so that the order in which my students learned the techniques has changed over the years. The success of a particular program depended on whether they were able to master a certain number of specific techniques within a time limit. If I saw that the majority of students could not master them, I changed the order for the next beginners' class.

For the last seven or eight years, however, I have found that the order the techniques are now in has produced students far superior to those who graduated from my school ten and twelve years ago. For that reason I present the techniques in this book in that order.

After mastering the basic techniques, one-step sparring, kata, and the basic combination techniques that are in the first techniques chapter, you will advance to the following chapter and the more difficult stances, blocks, punches, and kicks (also in combinations). Then, after spending the necessary amount of time in mastering those techniques, you will go on to the most advanced techniques and katas in the third and final techniques chapter.

I have set up the techniques in each chapter so that you will learn how to build up your balance and muscle control on a step-by-step basis and progress from doing the basic techniques on an individual basis to performing multiple techniques while moving forward and back. In addition, before you

xii   THE COMPLETE KARATE HANDBOOK

start sparring in the dojo or in a tournament, you will do one-step sparring with a partner to first sharpen your reflexes and to test the various blocks, kicks, and punches against a real opponent.

From reading the preceding paragraphs, you can see that this book doesn't present karate as a mystical art accessible to a privileged few but rather as a craft that can be learned by most men and women and successfully used, with certain modifications, on the street as well as in the tournament ring.

For these reasons, I believe that this practical, down-to-earth guide can help you to become more proficient and successful at karate—no matter what belt you are—without incurring unnecessary injuries in the process.

Before you start limbering up, however, you should know where modern karate originated and where it's heading.

CHAPTER ONE

A Short History of Modern Karate

ASIA

The history of modern karate starts in the first quarter of this century, when Master Gichin Funakoshi fused together the shorei and shorin systems of open-hand fighting that flourished on his native island of Okinawa to form a new system that he called karate-do—the way of the empty hands. His followers called the system shotokan, which means the house of the willow or the house of shoto. (Shoto was also the pen name that Funakoshi used when he wrote calligraphy.) In the fusion process Funakoshi first compiled, then edited and revised, and finally continuously updated the two systems' various kicks, hand strikes, blocks, and body shifts until the day he died in 1957.

Prior to Master Funakoshi's system of karate, the martial arts were really only fragments. People didn't practice the dozen kicks and half dozen hand strikes as we do today. Students were taught only two or three punches or kicks since their master's knowledge of the martial arts was limited entirely to those two or three techniques. Consequently, everyone also practiced only two or three katas, this out of a much larger total that was never codified.

This situation existed because of the poor conditions of Okinawa in the last years of the nineteenth century. The people were poor and the roads sparse and difficult to traverse; consequently, few people were able to travel and when they did it was infrequent. As a result, what someone knew in one part of the island was rarely known in another part.

Martial artists were therefore limited to mastering the few techniques they did know. They became masters of the front kick and reverse punch, for instance, and practiced just those two techniques and the few katas that concentrated on developing front kick and reverse punch. These men then relied on their front kick and reverse punch to win their matches against opponents who had mastered their own two or three special karate techniques, such as flying kicks or side kicks.

The martial arts were known on Okinawa during the latter half of the nineteenth century as Okinawa-te, or the hands of Okinawa. There were two major schools of instruction on the island and each emphasized different qualities in their particular martial art. The techniques of the shorei school emphasized strength and power and were suited to a larger individual, while shorin techniques focused more on speed and mobility and were suited to people with smaller frames and less strength.

No one event occurred overnight to cement these two schools of thought together into one cohesive whole. The process evolved over a period of years and was the exclusive doing of a young Okinawan school teacher named Gichin Funakoshi.

As a teacher assigned to instruct in many schools in different parts of Okinawa, Funakoshi was forced to travel extensively and, as he did so, passed through the major centers of martial arts on the island. As a result, he was able to study under excellent masters from different backgrounds over a long period of time. After a number of years, Funakoshi synthesized the best elements of the techniques and katas that he was taught and created a new system that came to use sixteen katas for teaching his new style of karate. A master now had not only to know much more than ever before but was also forced to broaden his horizon in order to encompass the many new skills Funakoshi had incorporated into shotokan's sixteen katas.

By 1921, Funakoshi was so well known and admired that he was invited to put on a demonstration of karate for the visiting Crown Prince of Japan. His royal showing was impressive enough to earn him an invitation to present his shotokan karate at an exhibition of the martial arts in Tokyo the following year. After he performed, several spectators, including the late Jigoro Kano, founder of judo, approached Funakoshi and asked him to instruct them in his new art. He did so and postponed his return to Okinawa. Many teaching offers and honors persuaded him to stay in Japan, where he continued to develop and teach shotokan karate until his death in 1957.

Soon after Funakoshi's death, all karate systems—Japanese shotokan, Chinese kung-fu, Korean tae kwan do, and Okinawan goju-ryu—went through a second revolution. It took place in the United States, however, rather than in Japan, China, Korea, or Okinawa, for karate was taken out of the dojo and put into the tournament ring.

THE UNITED STATES

Competition in sports always reflects the changes that take place with the level of development in that sport and karate is no exception to the rule. It has changed—and grown—in the thirty-five years that it has been taught in the United States, particularly in the de-

cade of the '60s, in terms of ideals, teaching methods, and tournament competition.

Karate was introduced to the United States just after World War II by returning servicemen and Asian instructors who were sent here by their masters to spread the philosophy of karate to the West. But it took about fifteen years for karate to develop a following large enough to warrant setting up a national circuit that featured regularly scheduled karate tournaments.

The karate that was practiced in the 1960s was different in both style and substance from the karate seen today, primarily because of the type of people who taught and trained in the art and the ideals that prevailed in the karate community of the '60s.

Karate was distinguished in that era by its hardness, toughness, and the ideal of practical application. Every technique had to work. The people who came to the dojos were not interested in finesse; they were not even interested in competition. They came because they wanted to learn an effective means of self-defense. They saw advertisements or exhibitions that demonstrated the power of karate and the awesome abilities that karate gave. This, then, is what attracted them and made them search out and go into the dojos to learn the art of karate.

Unlike the increasingly popular appeal that karate now has for millions of Americans of both sexes and all ages, the small group of people who studied karate in the '60s were usually men in their twenties or thirties. There was little or no participation among women or children.

The instructors' attitude was: "You (the student) will do the technique the way I (the master) want you to do it. If I tell you to punch your hand into a brick wall, you will punch your hand into a brick wall; if I tell you to do push-ups on your knuckles, you will do them. No matter how hard the training, you will do everything I tell you. And if you drop out, you have absolutely no character and no sense of perseverance."

The instructors who taught in the few dojos

operating in the country back then were mainly American students of Japanese and Okinawan teachers who regarded their mission as something holy—a crusade rather than a business venture. In fact, at that time dojos were long on hours and hard work and short on publicity. They shunned commercialism to the point where they often taught for free those students who pleaded poverty.

They were strong, tough, and capable men—no-nonsense traditional instructors— and the idea of karate as a sport took a back seat to their belief that karate was a martial art. So, naturally, the rules that were formulated by them and used in competition reflected that philosophy. They believed that only applicable techniques were worthwhile doing. You had to fight hard. The judges wouldn't award you a point for coming close to someone's face—it had to actually hit to score.

Since the instructors didn't go out of their way to see that the American public understood what they were doing, the media more or less ignored them, preferring instead to cover judo, the "gentlemen's" martial art— until some example of karate's violent side erupted and then that was splashed across the front pages. When the media did cover karate on its own terms, for instance by televising a national karate tournament, they were usually still ignorant of what was happening and so fell back to emphasizing just its visually exciting and violent aspects.

An incident in the finals of the 1965 Nationals that was televised by one of the major television networks shows how karate and the media have changed since the 1960s. Mike Stone was fighting in the finals against his opponent while the announcer was giving a blow-by-blow account to the television audience. In 1965, however, karate technique was just beginning to develop. People were just beginning to fight from stances and put together combination punches and kicks, blocks, and counterblows.

Like nearly everyone else, Mike Stone fought in just that style: open hands, no

stance, walking around without any finesse whatsoever. So when he chopped his opponent on the shoulder the announcer excitedly described it as "a lethal blow that gave him the championship." The shoulder was not a valid target area, however. But the judges in those days were much cruder so that chop was considered a lethal technique that was scored as the decisive point in the match.

Because of this type of situation, you tended to get competitors who were short on grace and technique but long on the practical application of the technique. They were brawlers. They could get into the ring and knock you out—which is what the competitors used to do in the '60s. It was, by and large, much more bloody than any competition is nowadays. As a matter of fact, in today's tournaments it's unusual to see any blood at all.

There *were* rules, however. And the rules were usually enforced. But the way judges looked at a technique was different from the way judges look at a technique today. Why? Because the emphasis was different. If two people were fighting, but one showed clear superiority over the other by doing strong techniques, and he knocked out his opponent with a punch to the face, he was awarded a point. The judges wouldn't disqualify him because he didn't live up to the rules. Instead, they used to change the rules to suit the individual. They used to say: "This guy is a powerful karate man. I can't disqualify him. He showed superior technique. He showed superiority over his opponent. Therefore, he is the winner." Back in the '60s, the criteria were totally different from the ones used by today's judges. They wanted to see who was the stronger man—who could beat and defeat and incapacitate the other guy—not who could score on him.

One reason the karate of the '60s tended to be so tough and brutal was because competitors would be *ashamed* to throw weak techniques just to score a point. If someone was punched in the mouth (an illegal blow) and started to bleed, he tried to *prevent* the referee from disqualifying his opponent because he didn't want to win by disqualification—that is, if he had any sense of honor. Instead, he invariably said to the referee: "No, no, no, it was my fault. I made a mistake. I didn't block. I ran into the punch. Please let him fight."

So, even though the rules said no contact to the face, all of us felt that if our opponent punched us in the face in defiance of the rules, the fault was our own and we deserved to lose. It didn't matter what the rules said. We figured that we lost if we didn't block the shot. In a street fight we would have lost. And every one of the rules was always compared to just that situation: What would happen on the street?

Back then, people didn't differentiate between street fighting and tournament competition. To the karateka they weren't the two separate things we understand them to be today. At that time, street fighting was really what people trained for; tournament competition was just a little more civilized version of street fighting. In fact, a lot of people felt it was ridiculous to have any rules at all and there was a lot of controversy over that feeling.

There was one instructor in Chicago, for instance, who advocated a no-holds-barred style of competition. His name was John Keehan (Count Dante) and he was a very controversial figure in the '60s. One of his students ended up dying in a brawl between his school and another dojo. While he wasn't typical of the '60s because he was a bit extreme, he did have a great many followers who, while they sometimes objected to those extreme views, did like him more than the other people around.

He held a yearly tournament in Chicago that allowed anybody to compete—whether they were karatekas, judokas, boxers, wrestlers, off-the-street punks, cowboys . . . anybody! There were no rules. The only rule was that you had to knock out your opponent— whether you elbowed his jaw or broke his knee or stomped on his head or groin. There

was one criterion to his karate philosophy and one only: If you proved mastery over your opponent, you won.

This influence was very strong in the karate community in the '60s. So in order not to lose any credibility, the people who were trying to introduce rules that would be enforced and who were trying to give birth to the "sport" of karate had to give way to the extremists in many instances because there were more people in the '60s who were prone to accept the hard, tough, full-contact karate rather than the softer sports aspect. The sports influence, however, slowly took hold in the '70s, so that now in the '80s, with all the rules in place, you will hardly find anybody really advocating full-contact, bare-knuckle competition anymore.

In fact, there is a schism today because of that evolution. These instructors who were trained in the early and middle '60s look at all the champions of the '70s and '80s and say: "Ah, if they had fought in the '60s, they would have been killed, because we had much tougher fighters." It's normal to look backward and imagine that the good old days were always tougher and better. But it seems that the current champions are every bit as good as the champions of the '60s. Why? Primarily because, as the brutality of karate was toned down and the concept of sportsmanship was introduced, a metamorphosis took place and karate evolved so that fighters started using much more speed, much greater precision, and much sharper and more scientific technique.

So while the top champions of the '60s were perhaps tougher than the top champions of today, today's fighters would probably be able to defeat the best that the '60s could offer. While the present-day champion doesn't have the toughness of the old fighter, he has much more skill: His kicks, for instance, are sharper and higher, his body is looser, he understands more about muscle control, and he understands more about techniques because techniques are on a higher level than they were fifteen years ago.

In fact, it's very difficult to compare the two decades, or the three decades—'60s, '70s, and '80s—because you're dealing with an art that has constantly been changing. What *was* has gone through great change and has been vastly improved.

The people who are leading the present renaissance of karate are the young, educated American instructors in their thirties who are products of '60s training. While they came out of the rough training regimens of the '60s, they are also a more refined product, bringing together the extremes of both decades. It is easy to see their influence in the fighters in today's competition: They are tough competitors *and* great technicians.

CHAPTER TWO

Stretching Exercises for Flexibility and Strength

Before you step into a ring and start throwing punches and kicks, your body has to be loose. If it isn't, you can easily pull a hamstring or strain your back. Every workout must therefore be preceded by limbering up sessions that will loosen the muscles, get your circulation going, and create enough body heat so you won't pull, strain, or tear any muscles when you start working. If you don't stretch, you run the risk of sidelining yourself for weeks or months on end by ripping a stiff muscle as you perform a "simple" punch or kick. And even if you don't ruin a muscle, you won't be able to do any of the techniques well. Your reverse punch, for example, won't have the power it normally would because you won't be able to swivel your hips all the way around to deliver the necessary momentum into the punch and you won't be able to lock in the hips and legs the way you should. (By "lock in" I mean bringing yourself to a complete halt when you deliver a technique. By focusing your muscles correctly and having your stance properly aligned, you will be balanced and your body won't wobble after the technique is finished.)

To become proficient in karate, you *must* have a body supple enough to execute techniques all of which call for a combination of loose limbs and strong muscles. To that end, I have put down the following exercises that apply specifically to developing your musculature and loosening up your joints.

To get the most out of these exercises, perform all of them and perform them in a relaxed manner. Don't push or pull your back or your legs as you stretch and don't bounce up or down either. If you do, you only increase the chances of tearing a muscle. Stay still when you encounter resistance and let gravity move you forward or down, and when you feel it prudent to stop because of pain, do so.

Do the exercises in the order that they have been set down for they first loosen the muscles in your neck and shoulders, then those in your back, hips, and finally legs. You then do combination stretching exercises to loosen the upper and lower parts of the body together. It is prudent, therefore, for you to start at the top of your body and work down if you don't want to injure yourself before you start doing the various techniques.

In the beginning, do only twenty or thirty minutes of stretching every other day and work up until you can do them every day—especially before every workout. If you arrive late for a class, for instance, don't join in and start doing the techniques cold. If you do and try to throw a kick, you're just going to pull your hamstring. Forget about missing any new techniques; simply tell your instructor that you need to stretch and go off to the side to limber up for about ten minutes. Then—and only then—join the class.

EXERCISES

Neck rotation. Keep your hands on your waist and slowly move your head around from left to right in a smooth circular motion. Do this several times; then move your head from right to left. To further loosen up the neck muscles, just let your head first hang back, then forward, and then to each side. (*See* Figures 1 to 4.)

1

3

2

4

Body stretch. Clasp both hands above the head and stretch the arms up as far as they can go; then stretch them to each side. (*See* Figures 5 to 7.) Next, move the arms and hips all the way around in a circular motion from left to right and then from right to left.

6

5

7

Arm rotation. Rotate both arms in a small circle from back to front and increase the circle on a slow but continuous basis. Repeat the process and work it from front to back, keeping the arms moving in an ever-increasingly wide circle. (*See* Figures 8 and 9.)

Front leg stretch. The spine is straight. The front knee is way over the big toe. Extend the rear leg as far back as possible and drive the hip down as low to the ground as possible to stretch the hamstring of the front leg. Do this with both legs. (*See* Figures 10 and 11.)

10

8

11

9

Side stretch. Keeping both feet forward and parallel to each other, push the heels apart as far as they can go and bring the hips as low to the ground as you possibly can. Maintain a straight back at all times. The object is to reach the ground or come as close to it as you can—forcing the leg, inner thigh, and hip muscles to pull apart and stretch to their maximum.

After you move apart the heels of your legs to their limit, let gravity pull your body lower and lower to the ground, allowing the muscles to slowly but continuously stretch. This exercise will create greater flexibility not only for kicking, but also for strong, low postures and free and easy body movement. (*See* Figure 12.)

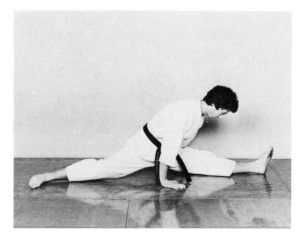

13

12

14

NOTE: By keeping the feet forward and parallel to each other as you stretch, extra pressure is placed on the inner thigh, groin, and back muscles. (This would not occur if the feet were pointed out to the sides.)

Front splits. The body is forward and the back leg is perpendicular to the front leg. Stretch out the front leg with the ankle turned up so that the hamstring and calf muscles and the back of the knee are fully stretched. As you slide the front leg forward, keep your back as straight as possible. After it is fully extended, push both legs in opposite directions. After pushing them as far as they can go, lean your head down and touch the front leg's knee. Repeat this exercise for the other leg. (*See* Figures 13 and 14.)

Double leg groin stretch. This stretch is especially good for side kicks and round kicks. Sit on the floor with the spine straight, your back firmly placed against the wall. Bring both feet together, the sole of one foot touching the sole of the other foot; then bring both feet in to the groin as much as possible. Move both knees down in a continuous up-and-down motion to either come close to or actually touch the floor. Once you have been able to move the knees down as far as you possibly can, lean your body forward (to put further pressure on the muscles) and bring your head down to the feet, both elbows pressing down against the knees. (*See* Figures 15 and 16.)

For the side thrust kick, extend one leg out at waist level. Be sure your heel is turned down and the hips, shoulders, and head are all on a straight line. To do this, you must roll over your hips and tuck in your behind. Keep your balance by placing your hand on the wall behind you and move the leg up with your partner by gradually raising it higher. Each time you increase the height of the kick, let it down half as much to allow the muscles to relax a little (*See* Figure 17.)

15

16

17

NOTE: Don't stretch forward from your neck or shoulder but from the small of the back or from the hips by moving forward from your chest.

Leg stretches against a wall. Another excellent way of stretching the legs for kicks is to lean against a wall and extend each leg out at waist level, slowly working it up.

NOTE: Don't force the leg up beyond the maximum exertion if you're in pain. It's also important to lower the leg as slowly as it was raised so the muscles can relax.

The same exercise can be done for the round kick by bending the leg back and then pushing the knee to the wall. Your partner then helps you raise it. (*See* Figure 18 and note above.)

19

18

To stretch for a front kick, stand with your back against a wall. Let your partner grab an ankle to ultimately bring that leg straight up while your hands hold on to the wall behind you for balance. (*See* Figure 19 and note above.)

Single leg pull/single leg extension. Sit with the left leg straight out. The right leg is brought back behind you at least 90 degrees, with the leg tucked. Push both the left leg and the hip as far forward as you can. Keep the left foot perpendicular to the floor; don't turn it to the sides. Now grab the left ankle and bring the body and the head down to the knee, all the while keeping the knee straight. Hold for up to forty-five seconds. (*See* Figures 20 and 21.) Afterward bring up the right leg in front of you and cup the right hand from the inside on the bottom of the heel. With your

20

spine as straight as possible, slowly bring the leg up diagonally toward your right side and straighten it out completely so the hamstring muscle is forced to expand to its fullest capacity. (*See* Figures 22 and 23.)

21

23

22

Double leg stretch. Sit on the floor and spread your legs apart as far as they can go. Be sure both knees are straight, not bent, and the feet perpendicular to the floor, not turned to the sides. Now lean forward and bring your head down toward the right knee. Repeat for the left leg. Now move straight forward between both legs and touch the floor with your head. (*See* Figures 24 to 26.)

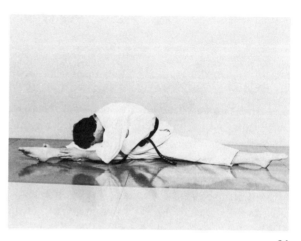

24

25

26

CHAPTER THREE

White Belt to Green Belt

People sometimes ask me why karate has a belt system and also why it has the color belts it does. First of all, except for white and black, the various colors in the different karate systems (yellow, green, purple, and brown) were arbitrarily chosen, even though "experts" will tell you that the green of the green belt symbolizes spring and that its wearer is now awakening, like the spring, in his or her knowledge of karate.

The white and black belts that were originally used separated the student from the master. The novice *and* the advanced student wore a white belt to show that they were pure and as yet untainted with knowledge of karate; the master wore a black belt to show that his karate knowledge was total and darkened with experience. As karate evolved, more belts were added to both separate the advanced students from the beginners and to let the students know exactly where they stood in their knowledge of the art. A yellow belt, therefore, knew most of the basic blocks, stances, kicks, punches, and katas; a green belt, all the basic techniques and katas; a purple belt, most of the intermediate-level techniques and katas; a brown belt, all the intermediate-level techniques and katas; and a black belt, most of the advanced techniques and katas. (There are also ten degrees to the black belt, first being the lowest, tenth the highest. These advanced areas are not covered in this book, which goes up to and includes the first-degree black belt.)

Besides aiding students, this system also benefits the instructor, since he only has to look at the belt a particular student is wearing to measure his degree of knowledge and ability. The instructor then knows what techniques to teach the student in any class.

For this book, I have compressed the belt system into three chapters, representing the three levels of learnings—basic, intermediate, and advanced. The basic chapter, therefore, contains the yellow, or high white, belt techniques and the intermediate chapter includes the purple belt techniques. Why break it down in this way? Because a yellow belt is still a beginner in what he knows and a purple belt is still at the intermediate stage in what *he* knows. If you look at the belts in this manner, the abstract coding of the colored belts becomes more comprehensible, giving you a larger picture of the entire karate setup.

When you first start learning karate, you have to improve your balance and muscle control if you want to perform the karate techniques well. Thus, in this chapter you will first learn the basic stances, punches, kicks, and blocks, do them in combinations, and then learn how to master them for "real" in one-step sparring—a prelude to free sparring—as well as in kata and bunkai. After mastering those techniques, you will start learning multiple techniques and the more difficult blocks, punches, and kicks (such as the crescent and round kicks). When you master all these techniques, you will then be prepared to tackle the intermediate-level techniques in the following chapter.

Since a white belt *is* pure in his or her knowledge of karate, it's important to make sure you don't make errors that can easily impede your progress if not immediately corrected. For that reason, you must know when to use speed and power, how to breathe when doing both individual and multiple techniques, how to body shift so that you are always balanced, and how to lock in on each and every technique. These four areas of knowledge are used in every belt level and how well they are done will tell you how well you are progressing in your training.

In karate, breathing—when to inhale and when to exhale as you deliver techniques—is vital to properly executing all the techniques; yet beginners often make the mistake of not breathing and holding in air as they deliver a punch or kick. Then, some seconds later, they exhale. This is the wrong way to breathe because the air inside the lungs will expand the chest and prevent you from contracting the chest muscles as you deliver a punch; consequently, you won't be able to put any real power into the technique because the chest muscles aren't being fully focused. It's important, therefore, that you exhale *as* you're contracting the chest muscles—just before impact with the target. After you lock in the technique, you inhale and relax the muscles, ready to deliver a second technique. It's vital that you learn to coordinate contracting your muscles with exhaling in order to maximize power in all your techniques—kicks, punches, *and* blocks.

Correctly using speed and power also involves the skill of breathing since whatever power you're able to put into a technique depends on two things—breathing and contracting the muscles at the right time. Many people, however, don't know when to contract their muscles. As a result, many beginners tense their muscles all the time and are forced to use power as they begin the technique—when it's not needed. When you tighten the muscles at the beginning of a technique you only slow down the punch or kick because you're moving against the force of the tensed muscles. This diminishes the power of any technique.

First, you have to reach your opponent as quickly as you can and *then* focus power into the technique. Therefore, you can relax your body and generate as much speed as you can into the punch or kick (which can only be done with relaxed muscles). Then, as you're about to hit your target, exhale, tighten the muscles, and lock in the technique. In this way, you get the greatest speed and the greatest power into the punch or kick.

For a beginner, it's always hard to know whether you're doing a technique well and whether your balance and muscle control are as strong as they should be. One way to test whether you *are* doing these things is to take a punch or kick and move forward with it at full speed. After you lock in the technique, see whether your body is completely still when you stop. If you were punching and your arm is wobbling, then you aren't in full control of your muscles. And if your leg or body is wobbling, then you aren't balanced. Now that you know what you're doing wrong, you probably want to correct it. But it's very difficult to be one's own teacher. Therefore, it's best if you have an instructor look at and evaluate your technique and help you to correct it.

Locking in a technique, as I said previously, means bringing your body to a complete halt when you deliver a punch, kick, or block. When you combine and focus breathing, speed and power, and balance in a technique in perfect harmony, you will be able to "lock in" and will see how vastly different it is from merely punching, kicking, or blocking. You increase your power tenfold and decrease your injuries.

As you encounter the basic techniques below and start applying these skills, you will see just how effective—and necessary—they are in mastering karate.

STANCES

Formal attention stance. This is the first stance you learn in karate. You use it for bowing in and out at the beginning and end of your class, kata, and sparring match. The spine is straight and the body erect. Feet are together and the hands, held open, are at the sides. (*See* Figure 1.)

1

2

Natural stance. The feet are planted on the ground and spread shoulder distance apart. The arms are held in front and to the sides of the body slightly and the fists are tightly clenched. The heels of the feet firmly grip the ground in order to lock the stance in. The body should be properly erect so that a line can be drawn from the heels through the legs and up the spine in a straight line. (*See* Figure 2.)

Natural stance, unlike formal attention stance, has practical applications for the kara-teka since you can do, with a few exceptions, all the blocking, punching, and kicking techniques from this stance. As such it is especially useful when you are being attacked and don't have the time to prepare to drop into another, more elaborate stance.

After a while, as you begin to understand how to root your body into the ground and combine the strength and sturdiness that your legs will get from natural stance, the front stance (or forward stance) will be the next technique that you will master.

Front stance. Start out from natural stance, feet spread shoulder distance apart, and move directly forward with either the right or left leg. The length of the stance is approximately two shoulder widths. The front knee is pushed forward and bent directly over the big toe. (Approximately 60% of the weight is on the front leg, 40% on the back leg.) The back knee is only slightly bent and the thigh and calf muscles are locked in to give the stance support. Standing with your spine straight, you should not be leaning forward or back, to the right or left, just perpendicular to the ground, the center of gravity traveling down from the body through the hips—which are always thrust forward. (*See* Figures 3 and 4.)

The heel of the back foot and the ball and toes of the front foot must be gripping the ground. This is especially important in front stance since you will be pushing off the back heel when you're moving forward and pushing off the toes and ball of the front foot when you're moving back. As a result, both feet must be properly stationed on the ground. The legs should be pulling apart in opposite directions (front leg pushing forward, back leg pushing back) to give the stance even more strength and stability.

NOTE: The practical length of the stance varies according to what it is being used for: A short stance is good for mobility and speed; a long stance adds to your power and balance. If the stance is too short, however, you will lack power in your techniques. Conversely, if the stance is too long, you will find it very difficult to move. (This applies to the back and horse stances as well.)

3

PUNCHES

Thrust punch. This is the first punching technique that a white belt student learns. Standing in natural stance, put the left fist straight out toward your opponent's solar plexus (knuckles up, palm facing the floor), right fist in the chamber (knuckles facing down, palm up, elbow tucked in). The chamber position is slightly above the waist, by the floating or lowest rib. Squeeze your right fist close to that rib. (The *fist* is clenched; the forearm muscles are not.)

Move your right fist out, rubbing the forearm against the ribcage, at the same time pulling the left hand back into its chamber. Both hands begin and complete their line of travel together so the body can tighten all the necessary muscles at the same instant to maximize speed and power.

Just before hitting your target, twist your punching hand around in a corkscrew manner so that the front two knuckles will be doing the striking. The left hand is also retracted in

4

5

7

6

a corkscrew motion as it travels to its chambered position. The left fist ends up by the lowest rib, with the palm up and the knuckles facing the floor. (*See* Figures 5 to 7.)

When you do thrust punch, relax the entire body but especially relax the shoulders, even though you may have to practice a great deal before you can control the muscles the way you want to. But when the shoulders *are* loose, you can then snap the punch out with the maximum amount of speed. Just before impact, as your fist is turning over, you prevent the arm from traveling further by tensing and locking in the chest muscles. In this way you combine the best elements of both speed and power.

I emphasize this again because too many beginners confuse speed with power; consequently, they don't know when to use speed and power in their technique.

When your hand is moving forward you don't need to tense the muscles and exert power, for locking in power before you reach your opponent not only slows the punch down but also takes power away from the technique. You need power only in the instant when you make contact with the target. That's why you drive the hand out as fast as you can and only at the last second exhale and tighten the muscles to focus the punch.

For any punch to work well, it's necessary to exhale as you make contact because exhaling forces the air out of the lungs and allows you to fully contract all the muscles. If you don't exhale, the air in your lungs will expand the chest muscles and prevent them from contracting. You therefore force the air out of the lungs by exhaling just as you make contact with the punch.

NOTE: In the beginning of training, you probably won't be sufficiently developed in your muscle control to always lock in the technique the way you should. This means your body might sometimes be carried beyond the contact point when you execute the thrust punch and will twist sideways as you finish the technique. If that happens, it will take power away from the punch by stretching the chest muscles out. The wider or greater the twist, the less tensed and focused the chest muscles are and the less power is delivered to your fist.

Warning. For all punches, make sure the thumb doesn't stick or extend out over the fingers of your fist even slightly. If it does, it might get broken because it will make contact with the garget before the fist does. Bend the thumb and place it over the first two fingers so that the thumb's inner edge tightly grips those two fingers below the knuckles. Remember that only the front surface of the index and middle fingers are used in striking.

Also make sure that those two fingers are parallel and flat and that the forearm and wrist are on a straight, even plane. This is done for two reasons: to prevent your wrist from breaking when your fist makes contact with its target and to get maximum power by having *all* the energy of the thrust both fo-

cused and moving in an unbroken line from the shoulder all the way down to the front two knuckles.

Moving forward.   To move forward in front stance, step forward off the heel of your back foot. Bring that leg in to the knee of your supporting leg in an arc and then out again to the side in one fluid motion to establish a new front stance. *(See* Figures 8 to 10.)

To move back in front stance, step back off the ball and toes of the front foot and simply reverse the path your foot travels when going forward. The reason you don't step directly forward and instead bring the legs together is to provide a small target as you're moving and to protect your groin with your legs.

Lunge punch.   This has the same characteristics as thrust punch, with one difference—a lunge punch is executed by moving forward in front stance, thus giving the punch the added ingredient of momentum. The punching hand is always on the same side as the leg that is moving forward. Thus, the right hand will punch when the right leg is moving forward and the left hand will punch when the left leg is moving forward.

As you push off from the heel of the back foot, make sure the front leg doesn't twist or move because the front leg becomes your supporting leg as you move forward. If your support leg isn't firmly planted on the floor, you might be propelling your hips forward properly but you won't be able to regain your balance or keep your posture.

As soon as the back foot comes down in front of you and locks the front stance in, you throw the lunge punch out (right arm) and lock the technique in, simultaneously bringing your other hand back into the chamber with an equal amount of force and speed. Remember to throw the punch out only after the front leg is planted on the floor. If your front foot *isn't* on the floor before you punch, you're going to be off balance and minus a great deal of power when you make contact with your target. (*See* Figures 11 to 14.)

8

10

9

11

12

14

13

NOTE: Don't stomp your feet as you move forward. Place them down. If you're stomping your feet, it means you're not moving forward with balance and your technique will be weaker than it should. In addition, as you move forward, don't let your body move up and down. If you do, you're going to lose speed, power, and balance, as well as making yourself a larger and more accessible target. Stay level in the stance all the way through the technique. Besides adding speed and power to your punch, it also prevents your opponent from knowing exactly how far or how fast you are advancing. His depth perception will be blurred by the fact that you are moving forward along a straight line.

Reverse punch. Unlike lunge punch, reverse punch is primarily a defensive technique. With lunge punch, you're moving forward to catch an opponent who is either moving away from you or is standing still. Reverse punch, however, is best applied when you're standing still and counterattacking an opponent, who is either rushing in or standing still himself.

With reverse punch, the punching arm is opposite your forward leg: Your right hand punches if your left leg is forward and your left hand punches if your right leg is forward.

Standing in front stance with the left leg forward, the right hand is back in the chamber and the right hip is brought back and turned slightly toward the right. Make sure the knees don't sag (especially the front knee) so the legs won't weaken your posture and balance.

As the right arm snaps forward and the left arm comes back, the right hip rotates forward. Use the spinning of the hips to gain added windup and put momentum in the punch. Then lock in the hips, arms, and chest muscles. That spinning of the hips translates into greater power, so how well and how much you spin your hips determines how effective your punch is going to be. (*See* Figures 15 and 16 for two views of the punch using

16

15

either hand.)

After you have mastered the individual punching techniques and then learned how to control the muscles so that you can bring them to a contracted position right at the moment of impact, you are ready to learn multiple punching techniques.

The first punch in multiple punching techniques always strikes the face. This snaps your opponent's head back and leaves his body wide open for your second punch. What you must remember, however, when doing multiple punching techniques is not to do the moves too fast or they will just be sloppy and ineffective techniques. You drive the first punch out fast, fully lock in the muscles at impact so you get maximum power into the technique, then do the second punch with the same amount of energy and speed that you put into the first one. You can't do *that*, however, unless you know how to breathe correctly.

As I said previously for individual techniques, you exhale as you contract the muscles when delivering a technique; next, immediately inhale and relax the muscles, then exhale again as you contract the muscles to deliver the second technique. Afterward, inhale and relax the muscles once more, and continue to breathe in this manner as you deliver additional techniques.

KICKS

Front kick. From natural stance, lift the knee of the kicking leg up to your own hip level, the foot tucked back and the toes curled up. Snap the leg out, bringing the foot up and out, and strike the target with the ball of the foot. (Keep those toes up so you won't break any of them.) Be sure you don't leave your foot out after kicking. You must snap the foot out and back in one continuous motion because the kick derives its power from that snapping motion. If you just throw your foot forward but forget to snap it back, you will simply push your opponent away with your foot. But when you snap your kick out and back, you deliver a full-force blow, since you will be snapping the ball of the foot off the target's surface—which allows power to be generated *into* the body of your opponent—and insead of simply being pushed away, your opponent will absorb the full impact of the kick. (*See* Figures 17 to 20.)

There are times when you won't be able to use front kick in a match or street fight, however—especially when the fighting is at close quarters and you simply don't have the necessary room to bring the foot forward to complete the kick. If you ever find yourself in that type of situation you simply forget about using front kick and use your knee(s) instead.

From natural stance, bring the knee up and out by driving or thrusting the hips out for greater power and sharper focus. This technique is very effective to the groin. Women find it effective since it doesn't require a great deal of strength to be able to deliver an extremely painful blow to a larger opponent.

17

18

19

You can also do severe damage to an attacker by grabbing his head and bringing it down, then snapping your knee into his face.

Stomping joint kick. Lift up the knee as high as you can, with the ankle and toes up and the blade or side of the foot turned down. *Thrust* the heel out and lock the leg in at the knee joint for maximum power. The striking area is the heel or the side of the heel, a very strong part of the foot. The best area to hit is the knee. Your target should be on an angle, either 45 or 90 degrees to your left or right. (*See* Figures 21 to 23.)

NOTE: This kick derives its power from the follow-through thrusting motion and, if executed correctly, can easily break your opponent's knee.

After practicing these basic techniques from natural and front stance in a stationary position, begin doing them while moving forward and back in front stance. When you're standing still, these techniques are much easier to

20

21

22

23

perform because transferring your weight and keeping your balance is not nearly as much of a problem as when you're moving to execute a kick or punch. When you're moving forward or back, however, you not only have to maintain balance while you're striking or blocking, but you also have to remain balanced while you're body shifting. And if you're not balanced while you're moving, you won't be balanced when you punch, kick, or block. Consequently, they will all be ineffective techniques. For that reason, you practice every block, kick, and punch while moving to build up both your balance and attack capability.

It takes several months of practice before a white belt begins developing a strong sense of balance and can then do the techniques properly and comfortably while moving. One surefire way of testing whether you're completely balanced is to move forward as fast as you can in lunge punch and then stop at the moment of impact with no wavering of the body whatsoever. When you stop, everything stops. You bring every muscle to a locked position. That is how you know whether you have proper balance.

As you develop your balance and muscle control, you will add even more speed and power to your techniques. For example, a lunge punch executed when you're a purple or brown belt will be totally different from the way you did it as a white belt—the punch will be more focused, the body will glide forward in a level stance, the spine will always be straight, and your motion will be more fluid. Every technique will be done better because by then you will be doing them instinctively, without thinking when to do what; consequently, the various elements will come together and flow as one.

BLOCKS

The various blocks now come into play.

Overhead block. This is the first block and is also called the head block. Start in natural stance, one fist in the chamber and the other fist straight out and pointing at your opponent's solar plexus. (For our purposes, right hand out, left hand back in the chamber.) *As you step forward with the left leg into front stance, drive the left hand out of the chamber, bending the elbow at a 45-degree angle as you bring it up and across the front of your body, ending slightly beyond your own head. At the same time, bring the other hand back into the chamber.* (You are blocking with the forearm, not with the wrist or fist. Your forearm must pass in front of the entire face, not just one side.)

As you snap your hand up, bring it overhead so you lift the attacker's forearm totally above your face, then lock in your arm and chest muscles. (*See* Figures 24 to 26.) At this point you also have to lock in the spine and the legs for more support—it's your entire body, not just your arm, that's blocking.

The guiding principle in all blocking techniques is *deflection*, not stopping or struggling with your opponent's force. You don't stop an

24A

24

25

26

27

27A

attack to your face; you move his hand a little bit above your head so that contact is made only between your two forearms.

NOTE: When you're moving forward or back, make sure the front leg comes down on the floor before you block; otherwise, you won't have any support for the block and will become unbalanced. Timing is also important here. The block should be deflecting the strike a moment after your foot touches the ground. If the block occurs too late or too soon, you won't be able to block effectively and will simply get hit.

Don't rise up as you're doing the block. Stay level in the stance throughout the block. Not only do you lose power if you rise up, you also have a good chance of missing the punching arm entirely and getting hit instead.

Chest block (outside block). In natural stance, place the blocking arm behind the same side ear. If you're left-handed, your left hand would be slightly behind your left ear,

28

elbow bent back. The other hand is straight out in front of you, at solar plexus level.

As you step forward with the left leg into front stance, bring your left forearm out in an arc, then in across your body, and pull the right hand back into its chamber. As the blocking arm makes contact with the attacker's punch, it twists so that the forearm and fist face your chest by the time the block is completed. (You get more power and sharper focus into the block through the twisting motion.) The forearm stops slightly past the solar plexus, blocking the upper body. You block with the inside or meaty part of the forearm. (*See* Figures 27 to 29.)

NOTE: If you don't twist the forearm as you make contact with your opponent's punch, you're going to be blocking with the bone in your forearm. This is not only very painful but can even break the bone in your arm.

29

Low block. This block starts in natural stance with the blocking hand behind the opposite ear. Since your left hand is blocking here, your left hand is slightly behind the right ear and your right hand is straight out. *As* you step forward with the left leg into front stance, bring your left hand out from behind the right ear and down across the body in a sweeping motion. Straighten the arm as you lower it, lock in the elbow, and tighten the arm and chest muscles. The block stops in front of the knee of the left foot. Any punch or kick coming to the knee or groin is deflected and swept out of the way by the forearm. (*See* Figures 30 to 33.)

As you begin using these blocks against "real" punches and kicks, you are probably going to bruise your arms. While this is something to avoid, you must realize that in developing the basics, you're going to inevitably make mistakes and bruise your arms from time to time. But in the process you will be developing strong blocking skills and the forearms will eventually build themselves up so that they can withstand the heavy contact that is inherent in blocking strong attacks.

30

32

31

33

You should now be moving forward and back in front stance doing front kick, lunge punch, and low, chest, and overhead blocks. (In moving forward or back in a front stance while blocking, the leg that's on the same side as the blocking arm is always "forward" with the block. When you do a right arm block, you move your right leg forward or your left leg back. When you do a left arm block, you move your left leg forward or your right leg back.) Doing all of your techniques in transition enables you to experience the sensation of body momentum, to combine movement with technique, and to develop your balance and coordination. You will also learn the advantages of moving and blocking, as opposed to just standing still and blocking.

If you were attacked with a strong front kick to the groin, for instance, the best defense would be for you to take a step back into front stance and do a low block rather than stand still and do a low block. Why? For the simple reason that you absorb that much more of the kick's power by standing still—even if you successfully block the kick. On the other hand, by taking a step back, you open up the distance between the kick and yourself, thus minimizing the degree of power you will have to absorb and the chance of hurting your arm.

KATA

The next area of training is something a great many karateka have unfortunately neglected—the performance of *kata*. Doing kata, however, is one of the best ways of learning balance, coordination, and muscle control.

The concept of the kata is very pure and very theoretical. You imagine you're standing in the middle of a room with a number of people who are attacking you from all directions. When you perform kata you're turning to the left, blocking, punching; turning to the right, blocking, body shifting, kicking; moving back and forth; retracing your steps—learning the balance, power, and coordination

necessary to defend yourself and counter their moves. Each kata teaches you a certain type of approach in handling a certain number of opponents and each is distinguished by its own particular philosophy and movement.

The kata for white belt level is the Takioka series. There are three kata in this series and all are important for your development. Takioka One uses all low blocks and lunge punches to the chest; Takioka Two uses all overhead blocks and lunge punches to the head; and Takioka Three uses inside chest blocks and lunge punches to the chest as well as low blocks and lunge punches to the chest. While Takioka One and Two use front stance only, Takioka Three, being a more advanced kata, uses a combination of both front and back stances.

Takioka One. This is the first kata in shotokan karate that you master. Its aim is to introduce you to doing kata by using only two basic techniques—the low block and the lunge punch to the chest. You move along a line that resembles the letter I, learning how to use the low block and lunge punch as a combination technique; for every attack is met by a low block and then countered with a lunge punch. In addition, Takioka One introduces you to body shifting between techniques on a 90-, 180-, and 270-degree axis and to using the blocking and punching techniques while moving forward.

Takioka One is started in natural stance. Your arms are held slightly in front of and to the sides of your body, both fists tightly clenched. Quickly turn your head 90 degrees to the left and move your left foot 90 degrees to the left a split second later. Establish a strong, deep left leg front stance and perform a low block with the left hand *as* you pivot your hips into the move. Thus, when your head begins its turn to the left, the left hand goes up behind the right ear; and as you body-shift to the left, the left hand sweeps down and across the body as you go into front stance/low block. (*See* Figures 34 to 36.)

34

36

35

When you do the body shift, snap your hips into it; don't just move your feet. *And* make sure your hands don't lag behind the body shift—the sequence is meant to be one continuous motion. Now step forward with the right leg and do a right hand lunge punch to the chest. (*See* Figure 37.)

After your right hand has finished the punch, bring it behind the left ear, at the same time quickly turning your head to the right to see if anyone is behind you. Then raise your right leg, pivot 180 degrees to the right on the left leg, go directly into a right leg front stance, and execute a right hand low block. Don't drop your right hand as you're pivoting. Bring it up again as you prepare to do the low block. You only slow down the kata and will probably do a weak block if you drop it. The hand goes up behind the ear and remains there as you pivot. When you block, it then sweeps down into a low block in one motion. Now, step forward with the left leg and do a left hand lunge punch to the chest. (*See* Figures 38 to 40.)

37

38

39

40

Quickly turn your head 90 degrees to the left, keep it there to observe your attacker, and bring the left hand up behind the right ear. Now lift and move the left leg and pivot on the right 90 degrees to the left to simultaneously establish a left leg front stance and do a left hand low block. (*See* Figures 41 and 42.) Now step forward with the right leg and do a right hand lunge punch to the chest. Step forward again with the left leg and do a left hand lunge punch; then, without pausing, step forward for the third time with the right leg and execute a right hand lunge punch to the chest with a loud, short kiya (yell). Kiyaing explodes the air out of the lungs and enables you to fully contract the muscles so that you can deliver the third punch with greater force. (Kiyaing is also an excellent way of scaring and temporarily paralyzing an opponent.) (*See* Figures 43 to 45.)

Quickly turn your head to the right and back, taking note of your attacker. The left

42

41

43

44

hand, which is in the chamber, then goes up behind the right ear. Now pivot your body 270 degrees around to the right on your right leg, momentarily exposing your back to your opponent, ending up in a left leg front stance and performing a left hand low block. Step forward with the right leg and do a right hand lunge punch to the chest. (*See* Figures 46 to 48.)

As you turn your head around over your right shoulder to note your attacker, bring your right hand up behind the left ear. Pivot on your left leg 180 degrees to the right to simultaneously do a right leg front stance and a right hand low block. After that, step forward and do a left hand lunge punch. (*See* Figures 49 to 51.)

Now turn your head 90 degrees to the left. Once again take note of your attacker as the left hand comes up from the lunge punch to behind the right ear. Then, spin your hips and step 90 degrees to the left, establishing a left

45

46

47

49

48

50

51

52

53

leg front stance and doing a left hand low block. (*See* Figures 52 and 53.)

Step forward with the right leg and do a right hand lunge punch. Step forward the second time with the left leg and do a left hand lunge punch; then, without pausing, step forward with the right leg and execute a right hand lunge punch with a loud kiya. (*See* Figures 54 to 56.)

Turn your head 90 degrees to the right and quickly bring it back, noting your attacker. The left hand comes up from the chamber to behind the right ear. Turn the body 270 degrees to the right by lifting and moving the right leg while pivoting on the left. Establish a left leg front stance and do a left hand low block. Step forward after the low block with the right leg and attack with a right hand lunge punch to the chest. (*See* Figures 57 to 59.)

The right hand then comes up behind the left ear while you quickly glance over your right shoulder to mark your attacker. Pick up the right leg and pivot on the left 180 degrees

54

56

55

57

58

to the right. Move into a right leg front stance and do a right hand low block. Now step forward with the left leg and do a left hand lunge punch to the chest. (*See* Figures 60 to 62.)

After you lock in this technique, pause a moment, then bring the left leg around 90 degrees so that you are facing forward and standing in the exact spot where you began. Return to natural stance to finish the kata. (*See* Figure 63.)

BUNKAI

After practicing Takioka One one-hundred times the karateka should master the low block and lunge punch. The karateka also slowly begins to develop more speed, power, coordination, and muscle control by constantly repeating the various low blocks and lunge punches *while* he is body shifting and moving forward. For these reasons, it is vital

59

60

61

63

62

that your karate training is accompanied by continual kata exercise.

But doing kata without adapting the techniques in the kata to their practical application is a misguided form of practice. Therefore, when you have done a particular kata a great many times, you progress to doing that kata in *bunkai*.

In bunkai you need several partners who act as the attackers and who throw the various kicks and punches at you when those techniques are called for in the kata. You defend yourself by actually performing the blocks and counterattacks that are also called for in that kata. If you fail to block the kick or punch, you will get hit. The motivation for doing excellent techniques is as simple as that. (Your attackers should step back when you deliver your counter techniques or else *they* will get hit.)

In this way, each technique is made real and you gain an awareness of how to apply what the various kata teach in a coordinated and disciplined manner. You are now on your way to using the techniques you learn in karate in a practical and efficient form.

The first move in Takioka One, for instance, is low block, so your partner will attack with a right leg front kick to the groin or stomach. You then turn, do a left hand low block to deflect the kick, and step forward to counter with a right hand lunge punch to the chest (which your attacker retreats from if he doesn't want to get hit). When you pivot 180 degrees to the right another student will greet you with another front kick that you block and counter. You then continue doing the various moves of the kata, with a student throwing the front kicks to match all the low blocks. When you do the sequence of three punches, your partner steps back from every punch you throw.

For the other katas, ask your instructor to tell you what each move in the kata is defending against.

NOTE: The fewer partners you do bunkai with, the more alert they have to be in order to meet you as you pivot and perform the kata's prescribed attacks. If they're too slow getting into position, they can ruin the pace of the kata and any benefit you may derive from doing the exercise.

Now that you know how to apply the basic blocks and punches, it's time you faced an opponent.

One-step sparring (Overhead block/reverse punch). Body and mind relaxed, stand in natural stance, feet shoulder distance apart. Your opponent is a foot or two in front of you in front stance, low block position. He will step forward and deliver a strong lunge punch to your face on your instructor's command or at his own discretion. You will step back a foot and block with the opposite hand.

If your opponent is attacking with the right hand, you will step back with your right leg and block with your left hand (and vice versa if he attacks with his left hand).

Timing is of great importance. Do not block before the attack has been committed

and only when the punch is about to touch your face. At that point move quickly and decisively. Bring yourself back a foot into a strong front stance. Balance yourself, snap the left hand block out and up, move the punch above your head, and then stop and lock the technique in. The right hand meanwhile has been brought back into the chamber. (*See* Figures 64 to 68.)

64

65

66

68

67

69

A split second after the block, explode with a right hand reverse punch to his solar plexus (remembering to stand still since you are in reverse punch position), hitting your partner as hard or softly as your instructor allows. Bring the left hand—the blocking hand—back into the chamber as you do a reverse punch with the right. (*See* Figure 69.) By bringing the blocking hand back into the chamber, you not only propel your reverse punch forward with that much more power and speed, but also

you can lock the punch out with greater focus. In addition, you can now continue your counterattack with a possible second strike with the chambered left hand.

Points to remember.
• Whether you step toward your opponent with an offensive or counteroffensive technique, make sure your front leg ends up directly between his legs. When that happens you disrupt his center of gravity. From this position, if he blocks and prevents you from hitting him, you can still kick him or cut off

his escape route by sweeping him off his feet. You can also hit him with great effect and ease with your knee to stun him and set him up for additional counter techniques.

If your front leg ends up outside his legs, however, you have given up this advantage to him and he now controls the situation. He can hit *you* in the groin or sweep you off your feet.

- When you step in deep toward your opponent, your punch is going to make contact with your partner whether or not he chooses to block or fails to block effectively. But if you step in and end up too far away from your man, then your techniques aren't ever going to reach him—block or no block.

- If you're not in a good, strong stance, your opponent is going to be tempted to sweep your legs out. Don't ever give him that advantage. Sink down into the stance. The deeper the stance, the lower your center of gravity and the more powerful the stance. Try to upset *his* equilibrium by trying to punch through his block and through him. Even if he blocks it, the punch will probably throw him sufficiently off balance to force him either to counter softly and inadequately or not at all.

- In one-step sparring, doing the techniques softly will not help you or your partner. If your attacks aren't strong, you do your partner and yourself the disservice of not providing an attacking "target" powerful enough to block against. He will not be able to develop *his* techniques and *you* will not be able to develop your techniques to their full potential.

Perform the same exercise using outside chest block/reverse punch (*see* Figures 70 and 71) as well as low block/reverse punch (*see* Figures 72 and 73). Consequently, the attacking punches will go to the chest and stomach areas. Don't favor your stronger side in one-step sparring, however, or in individual techniques either. Practice using both sides of the body so your weaker side doesn't become so weak through disuse that you stop using it altogether. If that were to occur, you'd be depriving yourself of half your attack capability.

70

71

As such, I recommend practicing one-step sparring ten to fifteen minutes during each one-hour workout, giving you the opportunity to apply the various blocks in actual attack situations. This sharpens your reflexes and sense of timing, increases your speed, and develops your body shifting skills so that you can move back and then forward easily in a balanced and decisive manner.

At this stage, you have trained six or seven months and have covered the techniques that

72

73

your reflexes aren't focused yet and your muscle control and balance are poor. To step inside a ring without having those areas developed to a certain degree, along with the confidence that comes with that development, is going to be a frightening and painful experience for you. The reason you study karate is to build up both your reflexes and your ability to respond instinctively to attacks with certain techniques and you will not be able to do that after only several weeks. To spar then will not only guarantee a high degree of injury for both you and your opponent but also it will hamper your progress or even convince you to stop your karate training altogether.

During your first six months you learn how to develop stances, how to develop more powerful punches through better muscle control, and how to improve your balance while doing the basic techniques. In each and every technique you will be combining breathing, timing, muscle control, and momentum to produce the maximum amount of speed and power of which you are capable. After six months you can start sparring with some skill.

Short of a street fight, sport competition is the closest you'll ever come to testing your karate ability, for it measures your self-confidence and presence of mind. Do you panic and go blank after getting hit several times? Can you stand up to a certain amount of pressure without falling apart?

In tournament competition your opponent is going to be more or less equal to you in training and ability, so if you miscalculate and miss on a technique, or if your reflexes aren't up to par, the chances of getting hit and injured are great. The element of risk is therefore ever present and that risk combined with pressure is what makes sport competition similar to fighting in the street.

Before you contemplate entering a tournament, first spar in the dojo against one of the dojo fraternity. Then enter a local event rather than a regional or national tournament to acquaint yourself with the tournament "scene." It's wise not to spar in your first tournament, however. Perform kata or don't

a high white or a yellow belt is supposed to have mastered. Once you perform these techniques to your instructor's satisfaction and are awarded your belt, you can begin to spar in the dojo.

I don't allow my students to spar until they have trained for six months because it takes that long to develop a working knowledge of the basic techniques. If you start sparring after only several weeks of training, it's as though you never trained in the first place—

perform in either division—just attend one or more tournaments to familiarize yourself with the tournament operation. When you know what to expect at competitions, then start sparring.

STANCES

Side stance.   Feet are parallel to one another and facing forward, spread two shoulder distances apart. Squat down as if you were sitting on a horse. As you do, push the knees out without letting the feet turn out and drop the body down in the stance. Keep your buttocks tucked in and the hips pushed in. The spine is straight and the chest out. (*See* Figure 74.)

To move forward in side stance, bring the back leg forward just to the outside of the front leg, which is stationary until the back leg touches down. Then the front leg moves forward while the back leg remains still to act as an anchor. The front leg goes forward to establish a new side stance while the back leg re-

mains as the back leg. (*See* Figures 75 to 77.) To move back, simply reverse the order in which your legs move.

75

74

76

77

If a line were drawn from the front leg to the heel of the back leg, the heels would touch to form the letter L. The heel of the back foot, therefore, must never go in front *or* back of this line or the body will be unbalanced and your techniques will be ineffective. Both feet are firmly planted on the floor, the toes grip the ground, and you lock in the calf muscles to give the stance added strength and stability. (*See* Figure 78.)

78

Unlike moving forward and back, stepping in side stance is a totally different maneuver since you bring your back leg forward, turn your body around, and continue to go forward with that leg after you pivot. The back leg comes up to just outside your front leg but doesn't touch down. As it reaches your front leg, you pivot around on your front leg, bring the back leg to the front leg without touching the floor, then continue to shift it forward to now become the front leg in a new side stance. To move back, reverse the order in which your legs move.

Back stance. Feet are at 90-degree angles (perpendicular) to each other. Bend the knees and sit on the back leg. (The back leg has 70% of the body weight; the front leg 30%.) The back knee is bent over the big toe while the front knee is only slightly bent. The buttocks are tucked in and the hips turned two-thirds of the way to the front. You are looking forward in this stance.

To move forward in back stance, simultaneously shift the back leg straight ahead and thrust the hips forward; then turn the front foot 90 degrees to the left or right (depending on which leg is in front) as the back leg comes down to now become the front leg in a new back stance. The front leg merely pivots to the left or right as you establish a new stance, it doesn't leave its spot on the floor. (*See* Figures 79 to 81.)

To move back in back stance, simultaneously shift the front leg straight back and

79

81

80

thrust your hips back; then turn your back leg 90 degrees to the right or left. As the front leg moves back into a new back stance, your pivoting back leg becomes the front leg.

PUNCHES

Horizontal elbow strike. In natural stance, fist tightly clenched, bring the attacking hand behind the opposite ear, then step forward into side stance and shove the elbow out and around in a tight arc. It stops at the same height as the shoulder, facing directly to the left or right of the body. The other hand remains in the chamber throughout the technique. (*See* Figures 82 to 84.)

This strike is useful as a side technique to the chest, face, and temple, with your opponent ideally situated on a 90-degree angle to your left or right. It is important that you keep the arm muscles tight and the angle of

82

84

83

the arc tight so that the point of the elbow pro-trudes out as far as possible, since it is this area that is going to be doing the striking.

Vertical and upward swinging elbow strikes. These come from the chamber position by the waist with the fist tightly clenched. For verti-cal elbow strike, bring the elbow straight out and up, again making sure the angle of the arc is as acute as possible. (*See* Figures 85 to 87.) For upward swinging elbow strike, bring the elbow around in an arc from the outside toward your target. The other hand remains in the chamber throughout both techniques. (*See* Figures 88 to 90.) The best place to strike your opponent with these strikes is under-neath and to the sides of the jaw, with your opponent standing directly in front of you.

Backfist strike. Stand in side stance. The starting position for your fist in this strike can either be behind your ear opposite the punch-ing hand or as shown in Figure 91. If behind

85

87

86

88

the ear, the fist is whipped out across the face and to your left or right side—similar to the horizontal elbow strike. The arm extends out but never locks and the fist turns over just before impact to allow the back two knuckles to strike. The other hand remains in the chamber throughout the technique. You don't let the back fist dangle after you strike; you *snap* the fist out and back as quickly as possible, never letting the arm or fist wobble. If they do, that back fist will be deprived of speed, power, and accuracy. (*See* Figures 91 to 94.)

The best areas to hit with this technique are the face, temple, and throat of your opponent.

BLOCKS

Knife hand block. Stand in back stance with both hands open. The thumbs are bent and placed on top of the hands, not in the palms. Pull the thumb back as far as you can and

89

90

91

92

94

93

push the fingers forward to create the tautness necessary for the technique to work.

The blocking hand is placed behind the ear opposite the blocking arm, palm facing the ear. The other hand is straight out in front of the body, palm down. To block, bring the hand down from behind the ear on a diagonal and across the body *as* you step forward or back into back stance, twisting the forearm and hand to expose the outside or knife edge of the hand just before impact. The hand will block at around shoulder height. Hand and forearm are both straight, the arm bent 90 degrees at the elbow. At the same time, the opposite hand will come back toward the body and twist around, turning the palm up, and stop at the stomach. This hand will rest against the solar plexus, fingers pointing along the stomach. (*See* Figures 95 to 97.)

The object of this block is not only to block an incoming punch but also, using the edge of the hand, to paralyze the forearm muscles as you block the inside of your attacker's forearm.

95

97

96

Unlike the low, chest, and overhead blocks, which are all done in front stance, knife hand block is executed only in back stance. So, before you actually block a punch, you must step to the side on a diagonal into back stance, placing your front leg directly between your opponent's legs, always doing knife hand block from either side with either hand on a 45-degree angle to your target.

Inside chest block. Stand in front stance, with the fist of the blocking hand tightly clenched and placed underneath the armpit of the opposite arm. The other hand is closed and extended straight out in front of the body at solar plexus level. Move the blocking hand out and up across the body to deflect the incoming punch, arm bent 90 degrees at the elbow on blocking. You twist the forearm and fist at impact so your forearm and fist end up facing you. While you block with one hand, the other hand comes back into the chamber. (*See* Figures 98 and 99.)

98

99

Inside chest block can be used to protect the face by lifting the arm up higher as you block. To protect the chest, extend the fist up to shoulder height only, the elbow close to your stomach as you block.

NOTE. *Never* extend the blocking arm beyond the body line; the farther away the blocking arm goes beyond this line, the less power and control you have over the arm and the less effective that block will be. The blocking arm must be bent at a 90-degree angle for the block to work. The more you open up or close the angle, the less chance there is of intercepting the punch since it will be either too far in front or behind the punch to effectively block.

KICKS

Side thrust kick. The striking area in this technique is either the side of the foot or the heel. In natural stance, bring the kicking leg up to the knee of the supporting leg. Point the kicking leg's knee toward the target. The ankle and toes are curled up. The spine and body are straight. (*See* Figures 100 and 101.)

Thrust the leg and heel toward the target and lock in the knee and hip, tightening the thigh and calf muscles on impact. Don't, however, bring the leg back right away. This is not a snap technique. (Don't leave it out too long either, for someone will just grab it and break it.) The secret of side thrust kick lies in how you use your hips. If you throw out and roll over your hips as you shoot out your leg and then lock in the hip as you strike, your kick is quite simply going to be devastating in its power. If you don't, then it will lack speed and the power that is derived from that speed; consequently, your leg will be pushing rather than kicking your opponent, causing him no damage whatsoever. (*See* Figures 102 and 103.)

After thrusting out the leg, rolling over the hips, and locking in the knee and the calf and thigh muscles, return the leg to the knee of the supporting leg—the chamber position—and

100

102

101

103

realign the hips and body. Then place your foot back on the ground. (*See* Figure 104.)

NOTE: In order to maintain balance in side thrust kick, you must relax the body and keep the spine straight at all times. When you're kicking, the body must bend away from the kick to allow the kick to rise to the necessary height. The higher the kick, the more the body must bend. Make sure, however, that you don't allow the bend of the body to throw you off balance and make the kick ineffective. To help you maintain that precious balance, always look at your opponent and keep both fists tightly clenched, the hand closest to the target straight out along the kicking leg, the farther hand bent at the elbow and kept close to the stomach. (The extended arm is also used to block your opponent's counter-punches.)

Side thrust kick can be applied to the knee, ribs, solar plexus, chest, and face of your opponent.

104

MULTIPLE TECHNIQUES

At this point, after you have moved forward and back in front stance and side stance, doing the various techniques you have already learned, you are ready to begin practicing the techniques in combinations. By continually practicing multiple techniques you improve your coordination, balance, and muscle control; and the combination of better muscle control, balance, and coordination will create a more effective technique and, thus, a more effective attack capability.

As you start doing multiple techniques, it's important to stress that the first technique *must* be totally completed, with the body brought to a momentary standstill, before the second burst of energy and movement can be applied to the next technique.

Caution. Before you attempt the first multiple technique—front kick/lunge punch—practice the front kick from many different positions; from natural stance (bringing the leg back into the same stationary position of natural stance); from stationary front stance (snapping the leg out and returning it to its original position so that you are still in left leg front stance with the right—kicking—leg back); and stepping forward in front stance (snapping the kick out, bringing it back to its chamber, and then stepping forward). Doing front kick from these stances and body shifts will enable you to do the technique much better because your balance will be stronger and the technique will be more fluid.

Front kick/lunge punch. As you go forward in left leg front stance, bring your right leg up and execute a strong front kick. At the moment you bring the kicking leg back into the chamber position, drive your hips forward, establish a strong right leg front stance, and as soon as your right foot touches the ground, throw out a powerful right hand lunge punch to the chest.

These are two separate techniques that, when done well, will seem like one fluid motion. You do a front kick, *stop*, and then perform a lunge punch. The more experience and proficiency the individual student has, the less time he will need to complete each technique. However, it is totally self-defeating for a beginning student to assume that speed in executing this technique is the most important ingredient in developing it. There is no question that in an actual street fight, fast execution is an important factor for its success. But in developing your skills in training, if you rush through the techniques without taking into account the fact that you might not yet have adequate muscle control, balance, and correct breathing, you will end up doing two very fast, off-balanced, and ineffective techniques. There must, therefore, be sufficient time *between* techniques to lock in every muscle before you start the second technique in the combination.

As such, the process of developing the necessary muscle control and balance cannot be rushed. At the beginning you must do the techniques slowly so that you can build up the coordination to first perform a strong and fast front kick, lock that technique in quickly and completely, then be able to drive out the lunge punch, lock that technique in quickly and completely, and come to rest fully prepared to do a follow-up technique, should that be necessary.

Front kick/reverse punch. This combination is vastly different from front kick/lunge punch since front kick/lunge punch is an offensive technique—you're advancing with the front kick to hit your opponent in the solar plexus, with the lunge punch held in reserve in case your opponent successfully moves out of the way of the front kick. If he does that, only your follow-up lunge punch will be able to cross the distance and strike your opponent.

Front kick/reverse punch, however, is capable of being applied both offensively and defensively since it prepares you for a different type of reaction against the front kick. From a stationary position in front stance, left leg forward, right leg back, attack with right leg front kick. Your opponent, however, has chosen to block your front kick and advance toward you with a counterstrike instead of evading the kick. At that point, you quickly place your right foot back to its original position, reestablish a strong front stance, and drive out a reverse punch to the chest of your advancing attacker.

This technique requires extra caution on your part because of the difficulty in coordinating the quickly shifting back and forth motions of the body: forward with the front kick, back with the kicking leg into a strong front stance, then forward again from a stationary position with the reverse punch right *after* your kicking foot touches the floor.

You have to maintain your balance while shifting your body first forward and then back on one leg, then be able to drive out a reverse punch with enough force to stop your attacker before he can reach you with *his* technique. All this requires a great deal of practice before you can develop the unique coordination that will make it work with both speed and power.

Reverse punch/front kick. From front stance, do a right hand reverse punch against someone who is close enough for you to reach with just the length of the punching arm. Your opponent chooses to move back and away from the punch, however, so that moving forward with another punch will be useless. What you do is leave the punch out and immediately step forward to execute a right leg front kick.

Now, if you've mastered these combinations, begin using more complex moves in one-step sparring.

Left side (inside) knife hand block/reverse punch. Your opponent steps in with a right hand punch to your chest. You step to your right side with your right leg into back stance, with the left leg directly in front of you and between your opponent's legs. Block the inside of his forearm with your left hand. Right after blocking, move your left leg (front leg) slightly to the left and spin the right leg and hip forward, throwing the weight of the back leg onto the front leg as you shift into a low, strong front stance. As you transfer your weight, throw out the right hand reverse punch into your opponent's chest, pulling the left (blocking) hand back into the chamber in a tightly clenched fist. (*See* Figures 105A to 105D.)

NOTE: How well you shift from back stance to front stance will determine how effective your reverse punch will be, since the momen-tum you gain by transferring your weight from the back leg onto the front leg, along with the spinning of the hips, determines how much speed and power your punch will have.

Right side (outside) knife hand block/reverse punch. Your opponent steps in with a right hand punch to your chest. You step to your left with your left leg, the right leg directly in front of you and between your opponent's legs. Block the outside of his forearm with your right hand. Now move your right leg

105A

105C

105B

105D

slightly to the right, body shift into front stance, and execute left hand reverse punch.

Knife hand block/front kick/elbow strike. Knife hand block can be done from either side, but in this instance, as the right hand punch to the chest comes in, step to your right with the right leg into back stance. Place your left leg between your opponent's legs and perform a knife hand block. Immediately after blocking, snap out the front kick with your left (front) leg and continue attacking by stepping into side stance to do a left horizontal elbow strike to your opponent's face or chest. (You can do the same techniques from the opposite side using your right hand and leg.) (*See* Figures 106 to 108.)

In order to improve both your reflexes and your timing in blocking and countering, in addition to refining techniques already learned, you have to use the basic blocks and counters in one-step sparring. Additional combinations are outlined below.

106

1. Overhead block/double punch (first punch to the face, second to the chest, from a stationary position).
2. Chest block (inside or outside)/double punch.
3. Low block/double punch.
4. Low, chest, and overhead blocks (separately)/front kick (kicking with the front leg—you transfer your weight onto the back leg after the block as you snap the front leg out—or kicking with the back leg). If you're doing front kick with the back leg, it's smart to grab your opponent's punching arm after you block for two reasons: (a) You will probably have to move back slightly with the front leg to gain the necessary room to execute front kick with the back leg and (b) by grabbing your opponent's punching arm after body shifting, you keep your attacker from escaping your kick.
5. Low, chest, and overhead blocks (separately)/elbow strike.

107

6. Low, chest, and overhead blocks (separately)/reverse punch.
7. Low, chest, and overhead blocks (separately)/front kick/lunge punch.
8. Low, chest, and overhead blocks (separately)/front kick/reverse punch.

BODY SHIFTING

Now that you have learned natural, front, side, and back stances, you start putting those stances together in combinations to improve

108

upon your ability to transfer body weight without losing your posture, balance, coordination, or power.

Starting from natural stance, shift into front stance, then into back stance, stepping forward and then back, shifting between the two stances with every move.

Next, shift from side stance to front stance and back to side stance as you step forward and back. After that, shift from back stance to side stance and move forward and back.

To increase the difficulty of the exercise, get into front stance, then step into back stance, then side stance, then front stance, then back stance, etc. Step back and repeat the procedure, making sure you shift into a different stance every time you move.

At this point in your training, it's important to maintain proper balance and good muscle control while shifting from one stance to another, or from a defensive position to an offensive position, because many of the techniques (especially the multiple techniques) that you are going to learn are based on different stances. As a result, the ability to adjust flawlessly from one stance to another is necessary if you are to learn and successfully execute the techniques. If this ability isn't there and you make an awkward transition between moves while struggling to maintain your balance,

you won't be able to deliver the technique with much power.

PUNCHES

Knife hand strike (outside). The striking hand is behind the ear of the striking arm, the elbow drawn back so that it is on a 90-degree angle to the head. The hand is open and flexed, the four fingers pushed out. The thumb is brought back on top of the hand.

Swing the hand out and around in a wide circular arc. Stop it when it is directly in front of you, striking with the meaty edge of the hand. At impact, the palm is up and the elbow is slightly bent. (*See* Figures 109 to 112.)

Knife hand strike (inside). This technique starts from behind the ear that is opposite the striking arm. The palm is turned down. Bring

109

110

112

111

out the hand in an arc; then straighten out the arm and lock in the elbow when the hand is directly in front of you, striking with the meaty edge of the hand. The palm remains face down. (*See* Figures 113 to 115.)

Insofar as this is also a circular technique coming from the outside in, these two open-hand strikes are effective to the side of your opponent's body—the jaw, side of the neck, and ribs.

Spear hand strike. The fingers are thrust out and the thumb is brought back on top of the hand. Hold the striking hand either horizontally or vertically at the chamber position by the waist. Thrust the hand straight toward the target and strike with the fingertips of the hand. This is best applied to the ribs, solar plexus, throat, and eyes. (*See* Figures 116 to 119.)

113

114

115

116

117

119

118

120

Close punch. From the chamber position, the close punch travels straight out and up, similar to a short hook punch in boxing. The front two knuckles are doing the striking but because this is a close-quarter technique that doesn't extend out fully as a reverse or lunge punch would, the fist doesn't have the opportunity of spinning around or corkscrewing as it makes contact. The palm is faceup as you extend the punch out. It remains faceup on impact. Lock in the biceps and triceps for power as you strike. On impact, the elbow is bent at a 90-degree angle. To maximize power, be sure the arm stays close to your own body as it travels out to the target. The other hand comes back into the chambered position as you punch. (*See* Figures 120 and 121.)

This is best applied either to the area directly below the ribs, if you are punching to your opponent's side, or directly underneath the solar plexus.

BLOCKS

Double arm block. Since there are times when one arm is just not strong enough to withstand the power of a strong kick, it's often useful to use two arms to block.

The left arm is blocking in this instance, so place both tightly clenched fists face down to the right side of the body and pull them back as far as they can go. The right arm juts straight back to the rear.

The left hand will travel out as an inside chest block from the waist or underneath the armpit. It swings out and up across the body, stops at the left shoulder, and twists at the last moment to turn the fist and forearm around so that they end up facing you.

As the left hand swings out, the right hand follows along across the body in the same counterclockwise direction and also twists at the last moment to turn your fist and forearm around to face you. The right hand will end up touching the left elbow joint, reinforcing the block. (*See* Figures 122 to 124.)

The right hand in this technique makes the block that much stronger because it doesn't withdraw back into the chamber as it normally would as the left hand shoots out. In ad-

121

122

123

dition, as you lock in the chest muscles, there is greater blocking power because *both* arms are reinforcing each other as they block.

Elbow block. Hands are on the hips with the fists tightly clenched, both elbows at right angles to the body. Move the blocking elbow around in an arc to move the punch across your body. The elbow stops right at the body line. (*See* Figures 125 and 126.)

KICKS

Side snap kick. The ankle and toes of the kicking leg are turned up to expose the side of the heel, which is doing the striking in this technique.

Bend the knee and bring the kicking leg into the chamber, which is at the knee of the supporting leg. Bend the supporting leg and keep the spine straight.

124

125

126

127

As if you were standing next to someone and wanted to push him away, work the hip and flick out the foot at the same time. Don't lock in the knee when you extend the leg. In this technique, the foot travels out almost to a fully locked position but right before the knee locks, the kick snaps back. (*See* Figures 127 to 129.)

As in all snap kicks, great emphasis should be placed both on the kick's speed and on quickly bringing the kick back; the faster you bring it back, the more power the kick will have and the greater impact it will make on your opponent. It's also important to execute the technique in a smooth, even manner by lifting the knee and snapping the kick out in one fluid motion rather than lifting the knee, stopping at the chamber position, and then snapping the kick out and back. Only then will the kick have the necessary momentum to work. The motion of the kick is similar to a whip that's lashing out and back.

128

129

130

Crescent kick. Crescent kick is a weapon that serves a dual purpose—it is both an offensive striking technique and a defensive blocking technique. In both instances, the arch of the foot is used in striking, with the ankle and toes turned up.

Crescent kick is best applied when striking a target to the side opposite your kicking leg. If your target is to the left of your body, you would use your right leg; if it is to the right, you would use the left leg.

You're kicking with your right leg here, so from a left leg front stance, lift the right leg up and swivel it across the body to the left, arcing the kick slightly yet keeping it on as straight a line with the target as possible.

The knee is slightly bent as you raise the leg and strike the target. After hitting your opponent, continue to spin the hips so that your supporting leg has turned 90 degrees to the left. Then bring the kick back to the knee of the supporting leg, similar to the chamber position of side thrust kick. (*See* Figures 130 to 134.)

131

132

134

133

You don't want to bring the leg up, hit the target, and continue to let your foot travel upward. You want to bring your kicking leg up to the height of the target, then swing across to the target and strike—similar to slapping someone's face. That's how you maximize the momentum from the swing into the kick.

Round kick. If you're striking with the ball of the foot, the ankle and toes are turned up; if you're striking with the instep of the foot, the ankle and toes are turned down. (The instep round kick, however, is the weaker of the two since it is similar to slapping someone with the back of your hand rather than with a closed fist.)

Lift up the kicking knee waist-high; then bend the foot and calf back behind the knee. The knee and ankle are horizontal to the floor and on a right angle to your body (chamber position). To kick, swivel the hips around in a circular motion from right to left (vice versa for left leg round kick) to snap the foot out and then back. Return it first to the chamber position and then place it on the ground. Balance is important in round kick so always keep the supporting foot flat on the floor. Don't let the heel of the supporting foot rise up at any time. You can, however, let the supporting foot turn around slightly as you're kicking to keep your balance. (*See* Figures 135 to 140.)

NOTE: When you rotate the hips, don't allow them to overpivot and turn all the way around. You can prevent this from happening by keeping your body facing forward for as long as possible, only allowing the supporting leg to turn around as you kick. This enables you to control the swing of the hips so that you can lock in the rotation and tense the muscles at your command, thus placing the kick exactly where you want it.

136

135

137

138

140

139

MORE MULTIPLE TECHNIQUES

Multiple techniques refine and sharpen your muscle control, balance, and coordination skills. Additional practice will teach you how to wait for that momentary still point between two techniques—after the first kick or punch has been brought back to the chamber and the body has just regained its balance—before you initiate the second technique. This is how you maximize the power of momentum from one technique into another in all multiple techniques, including the following:

1. Reverse punch/round kick
2. All blocks (separately)/double punch/ front kick/double punch
3. Knife hand block/front kick/reverse punch
4. Knife hand block/round kick/reverse punch
5. Knife hand block/side kick/reverse punch

These will help you locate the still point. They will improve your ability to lock in individual techniques and utilize momentum, power, and speed to their full potential. You are on the way to becoming flawless in the execution of the more difficult techniques.

POSITIONING

With the performance of multiple techniques, one of the most important ideas in karate now comes into play: gaining position for the next strike. Just to flawlessly execute a single technique is not the ideal in karate or any other sport (especially in contact sports). You also need to be in a position from which you can deliver second and third strikes that will reach a retreating attacker or a second or third attacker. As in pool, just to make a single difficult shot is useless—you want to sink as many balls as you can *in succession*. That means being able to make a shot and, upon completing it, be in a position to sink other balls as well. Therefore never let everything ride on any one technique that might also throw you out of position and render additional techniques useless.

Being able to deliver many techniques in quick succession is what tests the ability of a superior karateka. And when you can perform multiple techniques quickly with balance, muscle control, and proper breathing, you will know that your karate training has brought you to the point of mastery.

CHAPTER FOUR

Green Belt to Brown Belt

Now that you've trained for approximately one to one and one-half years and are studying at the intermediate green and purple belt level, you have certain responsibilities that you cannot neglect if you want to master new and more difficult techniques. This means you must continue limbering up before workouts, although you might not need as much time as when you first began. You must also continue practicing all the white belt techniques in order to improve your basic skills. Besides making sure that you don't become rusty, this will make it easier for you to master the green and purple belt techniques and katas since your muscle tone and balance will be greatly improved.

The following intermediate techniques are a combination of blocks and strikes that are either refinements on the more basic blocks and punches or are more sophisticated techniques that do the same job but in more select situations. The back hand strike, for instance, is a variation on the backfist strike; the scooping low block, a variation on the low and inside chest blocks. Such punches as the round and U-punches and such strikes as the ridge and palm heel are more delicate and fancier than the basic lunge and close punches. Consequently, they are used less often. The crossed-arm blocks and the slapping hand block are also sophisticated but delicate techniques that are used in fewer fighting situations. Nevertheless, you should know how to use them. You just never know when they'll come in handy!

The kicks, however, are new and more complex techniques that demand loose limbs and superb muscle control and balance in order to work well. You will also be going up in the air and skipping forward for the jump front, side, and round kicks.

In addition, you will master the sacrifice technique, where you fall to the floor and fight *up* at your attacker with kicks, and a takedown sweep that upsets an attacker and then finishes him off with a punch when he's on the ground.

There are over a dozen multiple techniques, an advanced kata, and half a dozen advanced one-step sparring combinations that you will master to further hone your reflexes and improve your fighting skills. Take care, however, not to overlook the multiple techniques, for at this level, developing kicking and kicking and punching combinations is especially important. Such combinations as round kick/reverse punch and side thrust kick/front kick gear you toward using a variety of hand and feet techniques and develop you into a more flexible and versatile fighter.

PUNCHES AND BLOCKS

Back hand strike. This is similar to the backfist in that you're striking with the knuckles of the back of the hand; here, though, the hand is open rather than closed.

Bring the striking hand behind the opposite ear; then thrust the arm out and around in a circular motion. Lock the elbow out and tighten the forearm, biceps, and triceps as you bring the back of the hand to the target. (*See* Figures 1 to 3.) The best area to hit with this technique is the temple or the rib cage, or any other spot on the side of the body.

Crossed-arm blocks. These techniques are referred to as cross-armed blocks since you cross your hands as you do the blocking. If it's a rising block it's referred to as an X-block and the hands are open; if it's a downward block it's called a wedge block and the hands are clenched fists.

X-block. Cross the hands so that they come to meet at the wrists; then thrust them upward to catch the forearm or wrist of the punching arm just where your wrists intersect to form the X. You push the punching arm above your head, using both your arms for leverage.

2

1

3

This block is useful if you want to grab your opponent's arm after it's been blocked. Therefore, if you're left-handed, your left hand should be on the inside of the block; if you're right-handed, your right hand should be on the inside. Placing your hands in this position enables you to grab and twist out your opponent's arm for control before you do your follow-up techniques. (*See* Figures 4 to 6.)

Wedge block. This is done with both fists tightly clenched. (If you're blocking down against a kick, leaving the hands open with the fingers exposed creates the distinct possibility of their being broken.) If you're right-handed, place your right hand over the left to form the X (and vice versa if you're left-handed). From the chamber of your right side, move them diagonally across your body to catch the kicking leg, and move it across to the side. (*See* Figures 7 to 9.)

5

4

6

7

9

8

KICKS

Back kick.   Back kick is among the strongest techniques in karate since it uses both the momentum of a full 360-degree turn and the spinning of the hips, which gives you that much more thrusting power. If you're kicking with the right leg, start in front stance with the left leg forward, right leg back. (Reverse the legs if you're kicking with the left.) Keep the front leg slightly bent for leverage and stability.

As you begin to spin around, lift the kicking leg up into its chamber, similar to a front kick, where the knee is up waist-high and the ankle and foot are tucked back behind the knee. (Make sure your spine is straight so your balance is assured when you make contact with the kick.) Spin the body around on the left leg 180 degrees so that your back now faces your opponent, but turn your head around completely so that you *always* keep your opponent in sight. Watching your target while your back is to your opponent, thrust the heel out and lock in the knee and hip on impact. Bring the kick back into the chamber, then continue to spin forward, and come forward to a front stance with the right leg forward and left leg back. (*See* Figures 10 to 15.)

Jump front kick (scissor kick). If you're kicking with the right leg, the right leg is forward in front stance. Bring the left leg high up into the chamber position as if you're going to kick, but at the moment the left knee reaches the zenith of its thrust, jump off on the right leg and execute a front kick with the right leg *as* the left leg is coming down.

You *must* have both feet in the air for the kick to work. In addition, the higher you thrust up the left knee, the higher your body is going to get up off the ground and the higher your right leg front kick is going to be. (*See* Figures 16A to 16D.)

11

10

12

13

15

14

NOTE: Remember to come down on the balls of your feet in order to prevent the shock of landing from traveling right up your spine from the heels of your feet. If you don't, your body will probably be jarred sufficiently for you to either lose your balance or reduce the effectiveness of any follow-up techniques through loss of both speed and power—not to mention balance.

MULTIPLE TECHNIQUES

The following sequences are good examples of both kicking and kicking/punching combinations:

1. Front kick/side thrust kick
2. Side thrust kick/front kick
3. Front kick/round kick
4. Round kick/front kick
5. Back kick/front kick

16A

16C

16B

6. Front kick/back kick
7. Crescent kick/side thrust kick (with the same leg)
8. Back kick/reverse punch (without moving forward)
9. Front kick/reverse punch (without moving forward)

These types of combinations initiate you into doing double attacking techniques while

16D

advancing. However, don't throw away the first technique in order to place greater emphasis on the second. Expect to hit your opponent with each technique. If your side kick lands squarely into your opponent's ribs or chest, then there is obviously no need for the follow-up technique. But work as though your opponent has evaded the first technique; this way you have the second kick or punch ready to go immediately after the first without losing any effectiveness in *either* technique.

Purple Belt

You have now trained one and one-half to two years and have covered a great many kicks and hand techniques, as well as the katas and multiple techniques that a purple belt is supposed to master. Once you do these techniques to your instructor's satisfaction and are awarded a purple belt, you start doing the following techniques. These punches, kicks, blocks, and stances take you into such new areas as jumping kicks, sacrifice and take-down techniques, other katas and advanced open-hand blocks and strikes.

STANCES AND BLOCKS

Hourglass stance. You are facing forward in this stance. Feet are parallel to each other and spread about two shoulder widths apart. The toes of both feet point in, the knees are bent over the big toe, and the weight is evenly divided on both legs. (*See* Figure 17.)

Scooping low block. This block is the opposite of low block. Rather than bring the blocking arm down across the body from the opposite side, you bring the blocking arm in from the same side—from the outside in. The arm

17

is straight in this technique. At the moment of impact, however, bend the elbow and bring the forearm and hand up to catch and then scoop the leg. You move the kick to block and then scoop for control. (*See* Figures 18 to 22.)

Slapping hand block. This is a loose, versatile, quick-movement block that doesn't require the rigidity and strength that are essential in most of the other blocking techniques. It blocks punches to the face and higher chest area best.

Stand in natural stance with both hands open. The right hand is blocking. As the punch comes in, the palm heel of the right hand comes in from the outside toward the punch and moves it across your body to the left. Right after blocking, the left hand moves in from the right with the wrist bent back and the fingers extended up and hooks your opponent's punching arm away, freeing the right hand for follow-up techniques to a now wide open body. (*See* Figures 23 to 26.)

18

20

19

21

22

23

24

25

26

27

KICKS

Hook kick. This is a powerful kick that uses the back of the heel for striking and is executed similarly to a side thrust kick.

Stand in front or side stance. You're kicking with the right leg. Lift up the leg, roll the hip over, and throw the leg out slightly toward the left. At full extension, move the hip from left to right to bring the heel directly back across the body (to the right), where you hit your target—which should be directly in front of you. To finish the kick, move the leg past the body, bending the knee back and hooking the leg. Your leg is now in a position similar to the chamber position for round kick. (*See* Figures 27 to 34.)

Jump (skip) side kick. This is a quick kick that is done from side stance. You're kicking with the right leg so face your opponent from your right side. The back (left) leg skips up

28

29

31

30

32

33

34

quickly to the heel of the right leg and as soon as it touches the heel, the right leg quickly shoots out the kick. You then lock in the side kick.

The variation from side kick is that the back leg is hitting the kicking leg out toward the target and propelling it forward.

Jump (skip) round kick. This technique is done best in front or side stance. The back leg shifts up to the front leg but before you transfer your weight, the front leg quickly snaps out the round kick.

PUNCHES

Palm heel strike. This is done best from front stance or side stance. The wrist is bent back and the fingers are extended up. The open hand shoots out from the chamber position directly toward the target. Don't allow the elbow to straighten completely, however. You lock in the muscles prior to having a fully locked elbow. (*See* Figures 35 to 37.)

The best areas to hit with this technique are the nose, jaw (in a diagonal upward movement), and rib cage (moving the arm and hand sideways).

Ridge hand strike. Since the four fingers constitute the striking area, push them forward so that they're taut. The thumb is placed into the palm. Place the hand in the chamber position by the waist, palm up.

Shooting the arm out in a slight, circular motion to the target, turn the arm over in a counterclockwise direction (if you're striking with the right hand; clockwise if you're using the left) and twist the hand at the point of impact so the palm is face down as the exposed ridge of the hand strikes. (*See* Figures 38 to 41.)

This technique is best applied to the rib cage, groin, temple, nose, and jawbone—the more sensitive areas of the body.

35

37

36

38

39

41

40

Round punch. This punch moves the same way as the ridge hand strike, except it's a tight fist that's turning over to expose the front two knuckles for striking. (*See* Figures 42 to 44.)

U-punch. Both arms are bent at the elbows, the lower arm's palm facing up, the top arm's palm facing down. The lower arm's elbow is close to the stomach, while the upper arm extends out a little farther.

The body must lean slightly forward as you deliver the punch. The technique comes from either the left or right side, from the outside in, both arms thrusting straight out and locking in the elbows as they punch and block at the same time. (*See* Figures 45 to 47.) For a side view and when used against an opponent, *see* Figures 48 and 49.

42

44

43

45

46

48

47

49

SACRIFICE TECHNIQUES

This technique is used primarily against a heavy and strong attacker or in the face of a knife attack, where you want to step out of the arc or path of the knife. Aside from that, the sacrifice technique can always be used when you want to quickly stun an opponent with an unusual surprise attack.

Stand still in natural stance. Your partner is attacking to the face with right hand lunge punch. Bend your left knee and fall forward on a 45-degree angle to the outside of your attacker (your left, his right), tucking the left leg tightly as you drop to the floor. The left leg doesn't move; it simply bends and the body falls forward on a 45-degree angle.

The right leg then comes up into the chamber position for round kick. Execute round kick to your opponent's rib cage or solar plexus. (If you want to extend the kick to the face, push your body off the ground with your hands, which will give your kick that much more height.) If your kick is sharply executed, your attacker will double over, giving you the opportunity to immobilize him completely.

Before he recovers from the round kick, place the right leg on your opponent's knee and the left leg directly in back of his ankle. Your right leg pushes on his knee, scissoring it between your right and left legs and breaking his knee. (*See* Figures 50 to 54A.)

51

52

50

The important thing to remember in this technique is not to move until your opponent has finally committed himself and has actually attacked. If you fall to the ground too early, your attacker can stop and nullify your move. Surprise, therefore, is the most important ingredient in making the technique work.

53

54A

54

NOTE: The more you resist falling down, the more you're going to get hurt. Relax the body. Allow the shock of hitting the floor to be absorbed over your entire body—the palm of your hands, the fleshy part of the forearm, the entire side of your torso, and your left leg. If you try to hold back, you are just going to pull muscles.

TAKE-DOWNS

There are many different types of take-downs in karate: The most common is to sweep your opponent's front leg out; the most dangerous (to your opponent) is to sweep your opponent's back leg out.

One of the most basic sweeps in karate is also one of the easiest take-downs to learn— and one of the most powerful as well.

In natural stance, block a right hand lunge punch to the face by doing left hand overhead block as you step back with the right leg into front stance. Slightly shift your left (forward) leg to the left so that you can step forward with the right leg into a front stance to the outside of your opponent's body (his right side), your right foot behind his right foot. As you're moving forward into front stance, grab his punching arm with your blocking hand and move it further out to the left to control it and pull him off balance at the same time. As you establish the front stance, your right arm also executes a strong horizontal elbow strike to your opponent's chest or ribs, stunning him and weakening his posture.

After finishing the elbow strike, open up your right hand and place the palm heel on your opponent's left shoulder for leverage.

You are now holding his right arm with your left hand and your right hand is on his left shoulder. Simultaneously push forward with your right hand, pull back with your left, and sweep with your right leg so you catch his right foot slightly above the heel, taking his leg out, upsetting his body, and throwing him to the ground.

Don't leg go of his right arm as you sweep and throw him down—that remains for control. (Your left hand, which is holding his sleeve, holds his right arm as his body falls directly before you. You don't have to take any unnecessary steps to reach him and thus lose both leverage and time.) As he falls, immediately bend down on your left leg and, coming to a kneeling position with your right leg, deliver a strong right hand punch that nails him to the floor. (*See* Figures 55 to 62.)

KATA

Purple to brown belt level katas are Tekki One and the Haian kata series One through Five. You'll see Haian Four here in detail.

The "Takioka" series of katas means "first cause"—or your introduction to kata training. The "Haian" series of katas, however,

56

57

55

means "peaceful mind," since the five Haian katas (which take you from midway to green belt to purple belt) teach you 80% of all the shotokan techniques. After you have mastered the five katas, you will have arrived at a peaceful mind because you will have great confidence in your ability to defend yourself.

Haian Four's purpose is to teach you a more advanced type of muscle control by hav-

58

60

59

61

ing you do the techniques very fast and then very slowly. Thus, you will do one move very slowly and gracefully, abruptly lash out the following move, then bring the third move to a slow and graceful finish before starting on the next series of moves. Haian Four thus teaches you to achieve muscle control not only by doing the techniques in one speed and then locking them in and stopping, but also by con-

trolling the muscles so that you can do the techniques well in a variety of speeds.

I have chosen to use Haian Four as the kata representative of the Haian series since it is the most indicative as well as the most beautiful of the Haian katas. In addition, many of the moves in Haian Four are repeated later on in the brown and black belt katas.

62

63

64

HAIAN FOUR

From a natural stance, shift left into a back stance, snapping your head quickly and sharply as you move. Drop the hands down, right arm out, left arm slightly bent. (*See* Figures 63 and 64.)

Slowly raise the arms up; then do an overhead block with your right hand and an inside block with your left hand, leaving both hands open. Now tighten the muscles. (*See* Figure 65.)

Quickly shift to the right. Without stepping, pivot your weight from the left leg to the right as you turn into a back stance. Turn your head to the right a moment before the pivot. (*See* Figure 66.)

Both hands come up slowly. Perform a left hand overhead block and a right hand inside block, leaving both hands open. (*See* Figure 67.)

Shift forward on the left leg and step into a left leg front stance. Do a wedge block (hands tightly clenched) with the right hand placed over the left. (*See* Figures 68 and 69.)

Step forward into a right leg back stance and execute a double arm block, right hand on top of the left. Shift forward with the left leg and bring the feet together, right hand

65

going into the chamber position. The left hand is placed over the right in what is called the "cup and saucer" position. Turn your head to the left. (*See* Figures 70 to 72.)

66

69

67

70

68

71

Simultaneously snap out a left side snap kick and a left backfist strike and bring them back. Extend your left hand out, palm open, then grab and bring your opponent's head toward you. Pivot your hip forward and do a right horizontal elbow strike, snapping your body forward to end up in a front stance. (*See* Figures 73 to 76.)

72

75

73

76

74

Bring both legs together, cup and saucer your right hand, and turn your head to the right. Execute a right leg snap kick and a right backfist strike simultaneously; then bring them both back. (*See* Figures 77 to 79.)

Extend the right hand out, palm open, then grab and bring your opponent's head toward you. Pivot the hip forward and perform a left horizontal elbow strike, ending up in a front stance. (*See* Figures 80 and 81.)

Simultaneously do a left hand low block and a right hand overhead block, with both hands open, as you snap your head forward. (*See* Figure 82.)

Pivot the hips forward so the left leg is in front; snap the hips counterclockwise and perform a left hand overhead block and a right knife hand block. Then do a front kick. Lift the right hand and do another front kick. (*See* Figures 83 to 85.)

Step into a short X-stance and execute a strong right hand backfist strike, with the left hand going into the chamber position. (*See*

77

80

78

81

79

82

Figure 86.)

Turn 135 degrees to the left and move the back or left leg into a back stance, the right leg now being the back leg. (*See* Figure 87.)

As though someone is grabbing you by your lapels or throat, bring both hands up in tight fists crossed over each other (right hand on the inside). As you settle into a strong, low

83

86

84

87

85

double punch. (*See* Figures 88 to 92.)

Snap your head to the right and shift the right leg forward to a back stance on a 45-degree angle to the right. Cross both fists again and pull them apart slowly, elbows close to your body, fists stopping slightly past both sides of the body. Counterattack with a left leg front kick and a double punch. (*See* Figures 93 to 97.)

You are now facing forward on a 45-degree angle, your right hand and left leg forward. Turn 45 degrees to the left and perform a double arm block, left leg still forward. Step forward with the right leg and perform another double arm block; then step forward with the left leg and perform a double arm block for the third time. (*See* Figures 98 to 103.)

back stance, pull the arms apart slowly to open your opponent's grip. The fists stop slightly past both sides of the body. You then counterattack with a right leg front kick and a

88

91

89

92

90

93

Move your left leg to the left and shift into a front stance. Raise both hands with the palms facing each other and grab your opponent's head. Bring it down to your knee, which is ris-ing up, to knee him in the face. (*See* Figures 104 and 105.)

Spin around and, as you place your right leg down, turn to the original starting position

94

97

95

98

96

and perform a left knife hand block. Step forward, perform a right knife hand block, then step back into natural stance to finish the kata. (*See* Figures 106 to 110.)

MULTIPLE TECHNIQUES

Multiple techniques at this level again emphasize both kicking and kicking/punching combinations:

1. Round kick/back kick/reverse punch
2. Ridge hand strike/round kick/reverse punch
3. Round kick/jump side kick (with the same leg)
4. Jump front kick/lunge punch
5. Jump front kick/reverse punch
6. Hook kick/back kick/reverse punch
7. Front kick/round kick/back kick
8. Back kick/front kick/round kick
9. Hook kick/round kick (with the same leg)

99

102

100

103

101

104

10. Front kick/stomp kick/round kick (with the same leg)
11. Front kick/stomp kick/hook kick (with the same leg)

The object of these multiple techniques is to spin the hips in the same direction through every technique in the combination. By spinning the hips in the same direction, you don't

105

108

106

109

107

110

slow down going from one technique into another. (You would, however, if you stopped and changed positions to kick or punch with the other leg or hand.) Instead, you not only speed up the delivery of the second technique but also you can kick with more momentum. All these things loosen the hips and enable you to deliver your kicks with greater flexibility, sharper focus, and greater effect. The looser your muscles become, the less effort you'll have to make in executing the techniques and the less chance there'll be of pulling a muscle.

ONE-STEP SPARRING

The best way to finish the chapter is to concentrate on doing the more advanced techniques you have learned up until now in one-step sparring. Listed below are combinations you should use to see how good you are at executing certain techniques in an attack situation. You can then apply this knowledge and develop a "tested" series of moves to use in free sparring. You then work on the techniques you are not that good at to bring them up to par with the others.

1. Outside block/elbow strike. After pivoting around on your leg to do an outside chest block, immobilize your attacker by doing an upward swinging elbow strike with the same arm to his face. (*See* Figures 111 and 112.)
2. Crescent kick block/side thrust kick. As your attacker drives in a lunge punch to

112

the chest, execute a crescent kick block that forces his punching arm to the side. Without putting your kicking foot on the ground, execute a side thrust kick to a now wide open body and face. (*See* Figures 113 to 116.)

3. X-block/front kick. As your attacker moves in with a lunge punch to the face, step back and perform an X-block. Then, holding his punching arm with

111

113

114

115

116

both hands, take a small step back with your front leg for better positioning for the kick. Then counter with a front kick to your opponent's ribs with your back leg. (*See* Figures 117 to 120.)

4. Knife hand block/spear hand strike. Step to the side and do a knife hand block as your partner attacks with a lunge punch to the chest; then shift into

117

118

119

121

120

122

front stance and counter with a spear hand strike to the throat. (*See* Figures 121 and 122.)

5. Elbow block/backfist strike. As your opponent advances with a lunge punch to the chest, perform an elbow block, hold the punching arm, and counter with a backfist to the face. (*See* Figures 123 to 127.)

6. Overhead block/stomping knee kick. After you block a lunge punch to the head, hold the punching arm, move the front leg back slightly for positioning, and perform a stomping kick to the knee with the back leg. (*See* Figures 128 to 131.)

7. Overhead block/side thrust kick/round kick/reverse punch. Step back and block a lunge punch to the head; then hold on to the punching arm with your opposite hand as you step back with the front foot for better positioning. Now

123

125

124

126

deliver a side thrust kick with the back leg. As you bring your kicking leg back, grab the punching arm with the other hand, then place your leg down and deliver a round kick to your opponent's ribs with the other leg. After you kick, let go of his punching arm, place your kicking leg down in front of you, and deliver a reverse punch to your opponent's chest. (*See* Figures 132 to 135.)

In order to bridge the gap from the intermediate to the advanced level, you have to continually stretch, practice the basic techniques, perform kata, and do both one-step sparring *and* multiple techniques. You should also be sparring now on a regular basis at tournaments as well as in the dojo to put all the techniques to the ultimate test.

127

129

128

130

If you train in this manner, you will soon find that your kicks, punches, blocks, and body shifts are becoming more instinctive and, consequently, that much more powerful. You are no longer wasting valuable time thinking about a technique before actually doing it. More importantly, you gain ever greater muscle and body control, improve your balance, and become more confident and aggressive in your fighting.

131

132

134

135

133

CHAPTER FIVE

Brown Belt to Black Belt

By now, you've spent anywhere from two and one-half to three and one-half years attaining your brown belt. You are about to graduate into the select world of the black belt. That means your techniques must be executed with the greatest speed, power, and grace. The blocks, punches, and kicks should be reflexive by now and you can measure how far you have traveled by thinking back to how you executed the basic kicks and punches when you were a white belt and how you execute those techniques now as a brown belt. Your breathing rhythm, your use of speed and power, your balance and muscle control, and your reflexes and timing are all on a more sophisticated level than when you were a purple, green, yellow, or white belt.

The techniques a brown belt learns in order to earn his first-degree black belt are the most advanced kicks and multiple techniques and advanced katas. Such stances and blocks as the cat stance and the chicken block are special treats in a regimen that demands you use your legs in such highly difficult maneuvers as the ax kick and inside round kick, in addition to the flying side kick and jump back kick.

Advanced katas, multiple techniques that force you to use the same leg for both kicks, and additional one-step sparring techniques that are on the black belt level complete your training.

Cat stance. Knee bent over the big toe, the back leg faces 45 degrees to the right (if it is the right leg) and holds 90% of your weight. The spine is straight and the buttocks relaxed.

The front leg is just in front of the back leg and rests only on the ball of the foot. Keep the front leg practically free of all weight in order to be able to quickly strike with that leg. (*See* Figure 1.)

Chicken block. In cat stance, bring the blocking hand up from the waist, blocking an attacker's punch with the back of the wrist and hand. Your fingers are pointed down and are close together. Bring your opponent's hand above your head and then do one of a

1

number of effective counters with the blocking hand. Since your hand is close to your opponent's collarbone, you can open or close your hand and bring it down on your attacker's face, collarbone, or arm—breaking his nose, collarbone, or elbow. (*See* Figures 2 to 4.)

Jump hook kick. From side stance, jump up in the air by pushing off with the rear leg as it comes forward, taking care to bring the knee of the kicking leg close to the chest before throwing the hook kick out.

Flying side kick. In side stance, the right leg is forward if you're kicking with the right leg. Step forward with and jump off on the left leg, bringing the right knee close to the chest before kicking. As you thrust out the right leg, the left leg will snap backward underneath the right kicking leg. Finish the kick, allow both legs to relax, and land on the balls of your feet and then your heels. (*See* Figures 5 to 8.)

3

2

4

5

7

6

8

Ax kick. This technique is done from front stance. The left leg is forward if you're kicking with the right leg. Lift the right leg straight up as high as possible directly in front of you. Keep the knee stiff and the thigh and calf muscles tensed. The ankle and toes are curled back. Bring the heel straight down on your opponent's collarbone, face, or chest. It's best applied to the collarbone. (*See* Figures 9 to 15.)

9

11

10

12

13

15

14

This kick's source of power is the weight you bring to bear on the leg as you bring it down on your opponent. Its best feature is the difficulty your opponent will have in blocking a technique that is coming down on rather than toward him.

Ax kick can be executed from the outside or inside with the same leg; that is, you can bring the right leg from the right side of the body straight up and down or bring it from the right side across the body to bring it down on the left side.

NOTE: If you don't lock in the knee and tighten the calf and thigh muscles, you might damage the knee. The entire leg has to be stiff for the ax kick to work well *and* safely.

Inside round kick. Inside round kick is the exact reverse of round kick in execution. However, you're striking with the same part of the foot, the ball.

Bring the kicking leg up to the waist, bending the knee and ankle back; then move it to the opposite side of the body. At that moment turn the hips and shoot the kick out in an arc from left to right (if the right leg is kicking; vice versa if the left leg is kicking). (*See* Figures 16 to 20.)

Inside round kick is best applied in close-quarter fighting. After punching your opponent, for instance, a quick inside round kick to the face is an extremely effective and applicable technique. Inside round kick to the body requires a little more distance for it to work well.

Jump back kick.   Stand in front stance with your left leg forward if you're kicking with the right leg. Jump off the ground as you're spinning around and extend a strong back thrust kick while both legs are in the air. Bring the kick back, continue to spin forward, and land facing your opponent. The kicking leg will end up as your front leg when you land.

16

KATA

From brown belt to black belt you have to learn the following katas: Jion, Bassai Dai, Kanku-dai, Empi, Hangestsu, and Tekki Two.

Once you get past the five Haian katas, all the remaining katas have a particular philosophy in overcoming opponents whose methodology falls into one of two categories: power or speed. The difference between speed and power is not that you're doing very fast or very slow movements; rather, it's at what point you tighten the muscles—at the beginning or at the end of the technique.

I mentioned earlier that to get maximum speed and power out of any technique, you first have to relax the muscles to drive out the punch or kick with speed; only when it has reached its target do you tighten and focus the muscles for power.

To help you attain this muscle control, the advanced katas have been broken up into

17

18

20

19

speed and power categories so that you can train to improve either your speed or your power. The reasoning here is that you will sometimes fight an opponent who is going to be quicker than you; therefore speed is going to be the element necessary for victory. At other times, however, you will be fighting an opponent who is stronger; power is then going to be needed.

Jion trains you to improve your power—which means that you have to tighten the muscles completely in every move throughout the entire technique, not only at the end. The muscles are therefore focused when you start the technique and you must drive the punch out with as much speed as you can against the added force of the tensed muscles. This will be difficult but it will improve your attacking power.

As you work on Jion, which is a relatively long kata (and part of its difficulty), your ability to quickly execute techniques with fully focused muscles will be tested to the limit. Jion is an important kata because of that.

JION

From natural stance, raise both arms, the right hand closed in a fist with the left hand open and covering the right fist. Bring both feet together and lower the hands down to slightly below the throat to begin the kata. (*See* Figures 21 to 23.)

Step back with the left leg and perform a double arm block—inside right hand block/left hand low block. (*See* Figures 24 and 25.)

Turn your head to the left. The left leg shifts forward on a 45-degree angle into a cat stance, while the arms cross and then slowly but strongly pull apart as if to open a grip that

23

21

24

22

25

has been applied to your throat. (*See* Figures 26 and 27.)

Step forward with a right leg front kick and attack with three punches—right, left, right—from a stationary position. Make sure you are in a deep front stance while punching to give you added balance and power. (*See* Figures 28 to 32.)

Spin toward your right to end up in a 45-degree angle to the right of your original position in a right leg cat stance (right leg in front). Cross your arms with the fists tightly clenched and slowly pull them apart. (*See* Figures 33 and 34.)

28

26

29

27

30

Step forward as you now perform a left leg front kick, then do three punches—left, right, left—in a deep, stationary front stance. (*See*

31

34

32

33

Figures 35 to 39.)

The right hand quickly comes up as you pivot 45 degrees to the left. In a stationary position you then perform a left hand overhead block and a right hand reverse punch in one continuous combination. The left leg is still forward. (See Figures 40 to 42.)

Step forward, do a right hand overhead block and a left hand reverse punch. Now step forward and do a left hand overhead block and step forward again and do a right hand thrust punch with a loud kiya. (See Figures 43 to 46.)

Step 90 degrees to your right, spinning on the left leg and temporarily exposing your back, into a back stance with your left leg forward. Perform a left hand low block/right hand high inside block. (See Figures 47 and 48.)

Shift your right leg forward and stand up in a natural stance to do a right hand close punch. (See Figure 49.)

Turn your head sharply to the right and step with the right leg into a back stance, performing a right hand low block/left hand high inside block. Shift forward with the left leg into a natural stance to do a left hand close punch. (See Figures 50 and 51.)

Step forward now with the left leg into a front stance and do a left hand low block. Open your right hand, shift the right leg for-

35

38

36

39

37

40

ward into a side stance, and extend a right
hand palm heel strike to the rib cage while

your left hand goes back into the chamber.
Step forward again, with the left leg, turn the

41

44

42

45

43

46

47

50

48

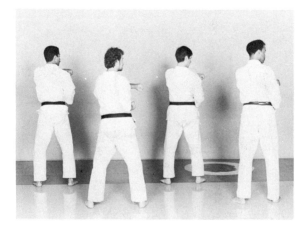

51

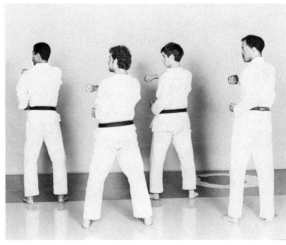

49

body, and perform a left hand palm heel strike; then step forward for the third time, with the right leg, and do a right hand palm heel strike. (*See* Figures 52 to 56.)

Move the left leg 90 degrees to the left into a back stance, leaving your back temporarily exposed, and do a left hand low block/right hand high inside block. (*See* Figures 57 and 58.)

Step up with the right leg and swing both arms in a high and strong double arm block. (*See* Figures 59 and 60.)

Spin your head to the right, step out into a right leg back stance, then do a right hand low block/left hand high inside block. (*See* Figure 61.)

Step up with the left leg and do a high and strong double arm block. (*See* Figures 62 and 63.)

52

55

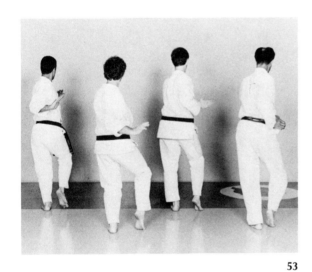

53

56

54

57

Cross both fists above your head and slowly
pull them apart. Pause, then bring both hands
into the chamber positions by the waist. The

58

61

59

62

60

63

right knee now comes up to knee your opponent in the groin. As you step forward into a very low X-stance (right leg is in front), perform a wedge block. Step back with the left leg and move both arms in a low block manner to either side of you. (*See* Figures 64 to 68.)

Step forward with the left leg and perform two inside blocks with either hand. Now step forward with the right leg and thrust both arms in front of you in a wedge block that hits your opponent in the throat. Leave the right hand out but bring the left hand back to the right ear. Then bring back the right hand and

66

64

67

65

68

swing the left hand straight out. Now drive the right fist down, breaking your opponent's nose. The right elbow is being held up and reinforced by your left hand. (*See* Figures 69 to 74.)

The left leg now turns 270 degrees to the right, momentarily exposing your back, as you pivot into a front stance and do a left hand inside block. Step forward and do a right hand lunge punch to the chest. (*See* Figures 75 and 76.)

Turn 180 degrees on your left leg (lifting your right leg) as you pivot into a right leg front stance to do a right hand inside block.

71

69

72

70

73

74

75

76

Step forward and do a left hand lunge punch to the chest. (*See* Figures 77 and 78.)

Turn 90 degrees to the left as you shift into a left leg front stance to do a left hand low block. Lift the right hand and right leg in a crescent kick-type movement and come down in a deep side stance, bringing the back knuckles of your right hand down on your opponent's nose. Perform the same technique with the left hand and left leg; then lift the right hand and right leg and do it a third time. (*See* Figures 79 to 85.)

Lift your right leg and pivot on the left leg 270 degrees into a side stance. Pull your left hand back into the chamber while the right palm goes past the body to block and then grab your attacker's arm. Pull your right hand back to the right side of your chest in a

77

78

79

80

81

82

83

84

tight fist while extending a left hand punch to the chest of your opponent. (*See* Figures 86 to 87.)

Shift slightly to the right with both feet. As

85

you pull the right hand back into the chamber, the left hand comes open. Block and then grab your attacker's arm with your left hand. Then drive the right fist out with a loud kiya, left hand closed into a fist as it is drawn back to the middle of your chest. (*See* Figures 88 and 89.)

The right leg and hand come back, hands and feet together, to the original starting position. Finish the kata by stepping to your left with the left leg into natural stance. (*See* Figures 90 and 91.

MULTIPLE TECHNIQUES

Multiple techniques that you should do at this level are the following:

1. Jump hook kick/backfist

86

88

87

89

90

91

2. Jump back kick/reverse punch
3. Front kick/ax kick

The following three combination techniques are done with the same leg. (You can put your kicking foot down between kicks as you shift forward.)

1. Round kick/shift forward/hook kick
2. Hook kick/shift forward/round kick
3. Back kick/hook kick

ONE STEP SPARRING

The one-step sparring combinations listed below are the most advanced and demanding of those outlined in the book. They not only involve executing sophisticated and powerful techniques, but also they force you to body shift quickly and well in a small area; this is necessary in order for the remaining techniques to work at all. In addition, the number of techniques required in each set is longer than in previous one-step combinations, increasing the chances of failure.

1. Knife hand block/elbow break/elbow strike. Step to the side to perform a knife hand block against a lunge punch to the chest; then shift into a front stance. Take your other hand and bring it in behind your attacker's punching arm. Bring your arm back sharply against your opponent's elbow and break it, using your blocking hand to provide leverage on the punching arm. Now bring your arm under your opponent's broken arm and raise it high above your head in a tight fist. Holding on to your opponent's punching arm with your blocking hand, do an elbow strike to his back. (See Figures 92 to 96.)
2. Low block/ridge hand strike. Defend yourself against a punch to the stomach with a low block; then counter with a ridge hand strike to the side of your attacker's head. (See Figures 97 and 98.)
3. Drop to knee/deliver punch to break knee. As your attacker comes in with a lunge punch to your head, drop to one knee and break the knee of his front leg with a bottom-fist strike. (See Figures 99 to 101.)
4. Low block/reverse punch/sweep/stomp kick. Immediately after you execute a low block against a front kick to your stomach, do a reverse punch to your attacker's midsection while holding his kicking leg with your blocking arm.

92

94

93

95

Move in with your back leg, simultaneously grabbing his jacket with your free
hand and bringing your back leg behind
his back leg to sweep him to the ground.
Finish him off by delivering a stomp
kick to his groin. (*See* Figures 102 to
105.)

5. Low block/knife hand strike/grab and
rip. Do a low block against a lunge

punch to your stomach, counter with a
knife hand strike to the testicles, then
grab the testicles and rip. (*See* Figures
106 to 109.)

6. Overhead block/hook kick/turn/hook
kick. Step back and do an overhead
block against a punch to your face.
Next, move your front leg back for better positioning and grab your attacker's

96

98

97

99

punching arm with your other hand, bringing your blocking hand back into the chamber. Counter with a hook kick to the back of your opponent's neck using your back leg and pivot around on your kicking leg after you bring it down. Grab your attacker's punching arm and then deliver another hook kick to his chest or face. (*See* Figures 110 to 114.)

7. Slapping hand block/elbow strike. Defend yourself against a lunge punch to the face with a slapping hand block and follow it by stepping in to your attacker and delivering an elbow strike to his face. (*See* Figures 115 to 118.)

8. Overhead block/round kick/palm heel strike. Step back and do an overhead block against a punch to your face; then

100

102

101

103

grab your attacker's punching arm with your other hand as you step back with your front leg for better positioning for the kick. Next, do a round kick to your opponent's midsection or chest with the back leg. After you bring the kicking leg down, step in to your opponent and deliver a palm heel strike to his ribs. (See Figures 119 to 121.)

At this stage, you have to pay attention to perfecting all the katas—from white belt all the way to black belt. Extra care and effort, however, must be made on the katas from brown belt to black belt. Insofar as there are six katas required on this level, you might have to spend up to two years in making the transition from brown belt to first-degree black belt. During this time, all the tech-

104

106

105

107

niques you have learned must also be perfected and the body made strong and flexible so that you can do all the techniques with ease.

When your instructor awards you your black belt, you will realize that in karate it's not what you know but how you know it that is important.

A green belt, for example, has learned

108

109

112

110

113

111

114

115

117

116

118

enough techniques and mastered them sufficiently to be able to do a tremendous amount of
damage to an opponent, but he is still young
in his karate development. His level of confidence is not that great and when he is attacked, he will probably panic and perform
"overkill" to compensate for his fear.

A green belt, therefore, is a very dangerous
person to fight because he has enough power

and technique to maim but not yet enough
poise and confidence in his ability to know
how many kicks and what kinds of kicks with
which to hit a person. He will instead unleash
all of his knowledge when attacked because he
is still developing his karate. Consequently,
he will hurt an opponent way out of propor-
tion to what is necessary to stop him.

A brown belt, of course, has advanced to

119

120

121

the point where his physical technique is near flawless and his confidence is great. This means that when a brown belt fights, he will execute only as many techniques as is necessary since he instinctively knows, after three or four years, the resistance his techniques will meet and what effect they are having on his opponent. He is able to *feel* the damage he is doing to an attacker and because of that he is able to moderate his attack.

A black belt, on the other hand, is a totally different individual. If a black belt has been properly trained, he will not like to fight because he knows the awesome power he has and is fully aware of the responsibility that goes with that kind of power. He will, therefore, be slow to anger and reluctant to fight.

Of course, when a black belt does fight, he knows beforehand whether he wants to break his opponent's left ribs or his right knee. He also knows if he should instinctively react with a round kick from his left leg or whether a slap in the face might accomplish the same results.

Physically and mentally, the black belt karateka has enough form, balance, and muscle control to deliver quick kill techniques. His ability to combine speed and power is so great that he can destroy his opponent with a single blow—and that ability is what *you* are training for. When he reaches that ultimate level of technique and its accompanying level of confidence, he can modify his attack according to the situation and use less power if he has to. Unfortunately, a great many karateka are trained to use a lesser amount of power when they train. The result is their inability to increase their power when it is necessary and the panic that comes of incompetence becomes an inevitable reaction to strong attacks.

Thus, at the black belt level, we have an individual who, because he is a trained killer, knows when to kill, when to maim, and when not to strike.

CHAPTER SIX

Kata in Tournament Competition

Unlike the kata you do in the dojo for your instructor to meet the requirements for a new belt, performing kata in tournament competition is something you have to train for in special ways. Longer and harder practice hours with more criticism from your instructor is only the beginning. Don't mess yourself up mentally in this area, however. Approach training for kata competition with the same dedication you take in training for sparring for attitude is often that extra little "thing" that separates a world champion from an also-ran. In this, as in the rest of your karate training, you must put in the hours and the effort in order to succeed.

There are six essential areas you must master before you can enter a tournament. One is the floor where you are going to perform your kata. The second is not to get mixed up about your direction. The third is pacing; the fourth, bunkai; and the fifth, proper ring decorum. The sixth and final area is being thoroughly acquainted with the rules and scoring system of the tournament where you're competing. This is extremely important because many tournaments—both regional and national—have significant differences in the rules and procedures so that ignorance can needlessly hurt you in the standings. Always ask your instructor to explain whether an upcoming tournament has any "surprises" you should know about.

THE FLOOR

Do you know the type of floor on which you're going to perform your kata? The question seems irrelevant and therefore of no concern. If that is what you think, you're making a big mistake. I'll illustrate my point with a recent experience.

I coached the United States National Karate Team on a tour of France in March 1980. One member of the French National Karate Team was the French Kata Champion and, as expected, during the competition in Paris, he performed a picture-perfect kata—until he came down from a revolving 360-degree jump technique. At that point he hesitated longer than he was supposed to on landing. Despite that momentary lapse, he continued on and finished the kata to enthusiastic applause.

That tiny hesitation, however, kept him out of first place by a narrow margin. The spectators may have missed it but the referees correctly saw it as a break in the flow of the kata. They deducted from his score accordingly.

When I asked him after the competition why he stopped at that point in the kata, he replied that he had to stop in order to collect himself. The hard rubber floor he had trained on didn't prepare him for the shock of the tournament's stone floor and as a result he was forced to remain still for a moment to keep from losing his balance.

A harder or softer or slicker floor than you usually work on might not bother you at all—you might proceed to do a superb kata and win. But if your kata has you flying in the air in a jump technique and landing on a cold stone floor, you will probably find yourself as stunned as that great French karateka since you too won't be prepared to absorb the shock. (A reminder: You *never* land flat-footed—on your heels—when you come down from a jump technique. If you do, the shock will move in a straight line right up through your spine from the heel of your foot. You can break this "line" and minimize the shock by landing on the balls of your feet *and then* your heels.)

So find out the type of floor on which you will be performing your kata. It may not be significant—but, then again, it could cost you valuable points and a championship.

This brings us to my second point and an aspect of kata performance that is hardly ever pointed out to students by instructors. Some karatekas fall into the habit of standing in the exact same place and facing in the exact same direction every single time they perform a kata. You might stand facing the front of your dojo, for instance, with the dojo's mirrors on your left and its windows on your right, and become so accustomed to starting all your katas from that position that you panic if the windows are on your left or if there are no mirrors or windows in the tournament hall at all. You might lose your sense of direction, fall apart, and start mixing up the moves. At the very least you might question yourself. And when there is the least amount of doubt in the competitor's mind about anything, he is finished. When your concentration is gone, so are your chances of winning.

I cure this problem by taking my students through a kata in several stages. First, I make sure they know all the steps to their kata; then I have them practice the kata over and over again for three different aspects: speed only, technique only, and finally for speed, technique, and power—plus kiyaing on all the correct moves. When you take the kata apart

and put it back together again in this manner, you become more familiar with the kata's inner rhythms and feel more at ease when performing it. Soon, doing the moves becomes second nature to you.

After my students have performed this stage to my satisfaction, I have them do the kata again but facing different areas of the dojo. One time they will begin facing the front of the dojo, the second time the back, the third diagonally to their right, then left, and then to the left and right sides of the room. After that, I have them practice the kata in the dark. I turn off the lights, draw the curtains or blinds, and tell them to close their eyes. Doing a kata in total darkness not only develops balance, proximity sense, sureness of direction, and self-confidence, it's also exciting and interesting to do.

PACING

Now that you know how to do your kata on any type of floor and can start it from any position in the room, you should learn how to pace the kata—to plan your movements so that you both start and finish on the same level of strength and speed. Unfortunately, this is not as simple to do as it sounds.

There is the problem of stage fright to overcome—especially if you are insecure about performing in front of a lot of strangers. You might not be able to cope with the pressure and rush through the kata. If you worry the movements out, you won't really lock in the power of the techniques the way you should and, consequently, you won't perform the kata to the best of your ability.

Some people are so desperate to get off center stage that they put everything they have into the first few movements in order to impress the judges but their strength is sapped as the kata progresses. Their kata soon slows down and instead of doing good, strong moves, they finish their kata on a very weak note. (Or they speed up and display a very fast and sloppy set of moves.) This type of pacing only shows the judges that you're not familiar either with the kata or your own body—you don't know how much power and speed to invest in each move so that you have enough strength to last you through *all* of the moves.

Having gone through this myself, I can tell you that the only way to combat stage fright is to immediately take charge of the situation as soon as your name is called. Smartly come to attention, walk up to the edge of the ring, bow to the referee with a strong and loud response *(oos)*, then step into center ring. Now close your eyes and wait for everyone to calm down.

When the noise has died down, you can then prepare yourself mentally to perform your kata. However, before you launch into your first move, make sure all of the judges are looking at you and not somewhere off in space or are turned halfway around talking to someone nearby. That's not part of their job and you shouldn't ever accept that type of behavior from the judges. Your job is to do the kata; their job is to evaluate it. And if they're talking to someone while you're up there, then they obviously won't be able to do their job.

This means that you might have to stand there for a while before everyone in the hall settles down and the judges give you their undivided attention. In effect, you're forcing the judges to look at you. When you have the attention of the judges you're ready to do the kata.

To pace the kata correctly, do the first number of moves and the last number of moves very strongly. Why plan your kata just this way? Because you make the greatest impact on the judges if you conduct your moves in a certain manner. When you first break into the kata, the judges are getting their first impression of you, so it's very important that you *explode* into those first moves and immediately grab their attention. Those opening moves should be done well enough to wake them up, to make them think: This guy is definitely a good competitor. I have to watch this. I have to stay alert.

Toward the middle, however, the judges are getting involved with the kata and evaluating your technique rather than your personality, so if you need to take a breather, this is the time to do it. Toward the end, you're leaving the judges with the last impression of your performance. Right now they're thinking: OK, he's finishing the kata; I have to give a score. As a result, the last number of movements must be done very strongly.

This is similar to the strategy that professional boxers use when they fight more than one round in a bout. When you are only fighting one round, you can burn everything into that round because the fight is going to be over soon anyway. But if you're fighting five or ten rounds, you have to change your strategy or you'll wear yourself out. So you start out strong to impress the judges and your opponent. Then, in the middle rounds, you slow down the pace and coast. But toward the end you have to burn out the rounds once more to either mount up points or knock out your opponent. The strategy should be the same in training for kata in tournament competition.

As you are training and as you become more accomplished in performing kata, you will become aware that there are different levels of kata competitors. To the judges, however, there are really only two kinds: those people who live the kata and those who don't.

People who don't live the kata simply do a number of individual movements and call *that* a kata. Unfortunately, this type of kata performer is on the increase—people who perform a number of movements without adjusting themselves to the idea or theme behind the kata. This is because they don't understand what the movements are all about. Examples of this are karatekas walking through techniques, pausing at the wrong time, not kiyaing—lackadaisically doing a number of karate moves in a certain predetermined order. Kata, however, is very far removed from that.

When you perform kata, you're fighting. You are not just performing abstract ballet moves. You're showing the judges that if you were attacked in a certain way by five or eight or ten people, this is what you would do—theoretically. As I said earlier in the book: Each kata has a philosophy. You're supposed to not only learn the idea or philosophy behind each kata, but also, while you are performing it, be able to *show* that to the judges. If, for instance, the kata is one that emphasizes strength, you have to show strength in your movements. If the kata is very graceful and fluid, you can't show strength; you now have to show graceful, fluid movements.

You must remember that the purpose of each kata is to teach you how to develop your body to move in a variety of ways. Thus, each block, body shift, punch, and kick improves your ability to stretch or exert power depending on how well you do each technique. Once you understand what the kata is trying to teach, not only will you benefit from it physically, but also your interpretation of the kata will be that much more accurate and consistent.

This is why your instructor should explain to you what every move in a kata means and its purpose for being in that particular kata. (If he doesn't, then *ask* him.) The different moves will then no longer be isolated kicks, punches, blocks, and body shifts, but an intricate, intelligent fighting pattern designed to thwart specific attacks. Quite simply, this low block is brushing away a front kick to the groin and you are countering with a thrust punch to the attacker's chest. You then body shift to meet the next attacker who is advancing at you from your right, and doing another low block to deflect another front kick, and so on and so forth.

Unfortunately, present-day instructors and tournaments allow kata competitors to make up their own katas but don't apply high standards to judging them. As a result, many of these katas contain moves and techniques that have been "flashed" up to the point where they have lost any relation to reality or serious body development.

I have seen katas, for instance, where a person is sitting on the floor in a full-split position blocking punches and kicks and then countering. I just hope that if this karateka ever gets into a fight on the street, he never drops into a full-split to perform any of his moves because, obviously, he wouldn't get too far. Nevertheless, I see more and more moves in these "original" katas that have no connection to the real world but that consistently receive high scores.

BUNKAI

Partly for this reason, I bring the reality of kata home to my students by making sure they learn bunkai. Bunkai bridges the gap between theory and practice. You make the kata come alive by working through the kata. In bunkai, each movement in the kata is acted out by the kata performer with the requisite number of attackers who perform the attacks called for in order to let the kata performer do the blocks and counters for "real."

If you have to step to the left and block a front kick to the groin, an actual front kick will greet you as you body shift into a low block and you will have to successfully block the kick or be hit by it. If you block the front kick, you then have to counter to the attacker's chest with a thrust punch. You then body shift to your right to meet your next attacker, who is also coming at you in this particular kata with a front kick to the groin. You have to block that and counter and then body shift 90 degrees to your left to your third attacker. And so on, until you finish the kata.

When you practice bunkai a great deal, the coordination you develop in doing the moves is going to take on much greater significance. If somebody attacks you in Takioka One with a front kick strong enough to hurt you and you spin around to do the kind of strong block that will block the kick, the next time you perform that kata, you will not be able to do a weak block because you now know there is a kick coming at you. You have experienced that kick. You have also experienced the block. Now, every time you do the kata, you will always remember that experience and you will always do strong, powerful blocks. This means you will always have strong, powerful katas.

Since the kata is now removed from the realm of the abstract forever, your punches, kicks, blocks, and body shifts are going to have that much more speed, power, and intensity. That intensity comes with the full understanding of the movements and this is not lost on the judges because it shows them you fully understand what you're doing and that your concentration is 100%. When you perform a kata on that level, you assure yourself of getting a very high score as well as the respect and envy of fellow competitors.

GETTING INTO THE RING

After bunkai, you are ready for the final stage in your training: familiarizing yourself with the pressure that you will have to go through in a tournament. You are now preparing yourself for the intangible—being completely relaxed when performing a kata in front of a crowd. You can prepare yourself for this by duplicating a tournament "situation" in your dojo. If your instructor takes you and your classmates through a simulated tournament it usually eliminates some of your brooding pre-tournament anxiety and helps you relax just prior to competition.

Your instructor should be aware of all this. If he isn't, however, ask him to mark out a ring in the dojo a week before competition day and to stand facing the class. You either stand or sit in line, as you would at a tournament, and wait for your name to be called. When it is, don't dawdle but come to with a "oos," walk up to the edge of the ring, and bow to your instructor (judge); then walk to where you are going to start your kata. Bow once more, then announce your name, school, and the name of the kata that you are going to perform. When you finish the kata bow out, and wait for your score to be announced (in this instance, your instructor's suggestions on how to improve your kata).

This is the time to remember that your performance begins the moment your name is called and that your performance ends when the score has been announced. It's a mistake for you to think your performance is only going to be gauged on the kata itself. You are not dealing with five robots but five judges who are human beings; so keep in mind that they are also going to be affected by your attitude and how you choose to present yourself to them.

All right. Your name has been called. The judges are waiting for you to get up there and you're taking your time; you're fixing your gi. Finally, you decide that you're going to mosey into the ring like a superstar. If you do that, I can almost guarantee that you're going to get a low score because judges don't like to see that.

When your name has been called, snap to with a oos. Step inside the ring, oos. You're ready and you're showing a strong and respectful attitude. The judges will see that and say: good, strong attitude. Now, if you have a strong kata behind it you're in very good shape.

But if you walk into the ring and you're too arrogant, even if your performance is excellent, you're still putting the judges on the spot. Your attitude is telling the judges: "I'm only here because I'm a great star." It's obvious, then, that you have to show the proper decorum if you don't want to lose. But your kata must also be good; otherwise, no matter how superb your bearing, you won't get a winning score.

Think of yourself as a performer at all times because that is exactly what you are. Don't, however, get nervous and rush through the kata; perform your kata. Let the kata bring out your personality. And don't be timid. Believe in your kata. You should realize that you cannot convince anyone your kata is good unless you *yourself* are convinced of it!

SCORING

Your instructor should also explain to you the scoring system of the tournament in which you are going to compete. Usually five referees will judge your kata on a scale of 1 through 10: 5 and 6 are fair and average, 7 good, 8 very good, 9 excellent, and 10 perfection (and rarely given). To obtain the score, the highest and lowest numbers are often dropped and the remaining ones added up.

Every tournament you compete in will have those five referees. But when you have five judges in a ring who are not familiar with one another's judging standards, they are not usually going to see eye to eye as to just what constitutes poor, fair, good, and excellent scores. For that reason, one of the following two methods is usually employed at the start of kata competition to determine the judging standards for that day's competition.

The first method is to call up three kata competitors to do their katas. As each one finishes his kata, it is evaluated by the judges but is given no score. After the third performance is evaluated, the three competitors are then individually called back to the ring and awarded their score.

This method allows the judges to compare one kata against several others. In that way, they can usually come to a consensus as to what will be considered a superior kata, an average kata, and a poor kata. They can then award points that will make sense to the performers as well as to the officials.

The other method is to have one competitor perform his kata without being awarded a score at all. When he finishes his kata, the judges convene to poll one another as to what each one would give that particular kata. They discuss the kata among themselves and then they arrive at a consensus that will be used to judge every kata for the remainder of the tournament. Later in the competition, after the initial kata performer has had ample time to rest, he is called back to perform once more. At that point, he is given a score for his work.

Don't think all this information is useless to you. It's not. The more you know about the particular tournament you are going to compete in—its procedures, scoring methods, gym condition, etc.—the closer to victory you're going to be, since there will be that much less chance of the unexpected occurring to upset you or throw you off your mark.

Now you've finally finished your training. You have entered a tournament and are outside some gymnasium waiting to go inside. As you are waiting, keep this in mind: The moment you pass through the front door, you start competing. People will be looking at you, talking about you, evaluating you as a competitor. And you should be doing the same thing. In addition, if you can pick up any information on a referee's prejudices or a tip from a veteran on how to improve your performance, by all means grab it. Never go into a tournament and act deaf, dumb, and blind!

Kata competition is always first on the agenda, so be mentally prepared to compete as soon as you arrive. There will also be hundreds of other competitors there with you—all as psyched up as you to win—so don't lose your poise by letting either the sheer number of people present or their psych games get to you. If you allow yourself to be intimidated, you can lose the competition before you even step inside a ring.

Stay with people you know, warm up, and look unimpressed with the hubbub that's going on all around you. If you want, note the tricks that other competitors are doing and play it back on them. Psych *them* out; upset *their* equilibrium.

Here is one psych technique you can use to good effect. Walk out of the dressing room with a towel draped around your neck. Then walk up to the ring before the start of competition and check it out. Take the towel off your neck and wipe the ring clean. Let everyone know that you demand that certain things be done before you step inside a ring to compete. Then loosen up inside the ring for a while.

Claim ownership of *that* ring and make it work for you.

THE ESSENTIALS

Now is a good time to quickly review some of the basics of kata performing. A thumbnail sketch is outlined below.

1. When you do the first move, snap into it.
2. If you are in a deep stance, don't come up a little before going into the next move. If you rise up and down on different moves, you lose power, speed, and balance.
3. When you have to body shift and immediately do a block, make it one move, not two. Spin the hip and block in one fluid motion.
4. Feel your feet; don't look at them.
5. If you anticipate the next move, you won't be locking in the present move.
6. Snapping your head into place shows that you're alert and it dresses up the kata visually.
7. Don't pivot, *then* bring your hands into place. Prepare the hands so that when you pivot, the hands and feet arrive together. If you pivot and your hands are lagging behind, you might not be able to block a punch that's coming in at you. More important, to the judges it displays a lack of timing and coordination.

COMPETITION TIPS

Before you perform your kata, be absolutely prepared and at ease because anything you do after you enter that ring is marked and noted by the referees. Don't fidget or loosen up just as you're going to perform your kata or do anything else that might indicate to the judges that you're not in a strong state of mind. Get rid of any nervous tics or stiff joints on the sidelines while you're waiting for your name to be called. Usually your name will be announced twice: the first time to signal to you that you're "on deck"; the second time to call you to the ring to perform your kata.

All right. Your name has been called for the second time. You are eager, unafraid, and relaxed. Walk up to the edge of the ring and face the head referee, bowing to him with a strong *oos*. Then walk into center ring and again bow to the referee with a *oos*. Announce your name, school, and the kata that you are going to perform. Present a strong attitude and speak in a loud, clear voice.

Take a deep breath, close your eyes, and collect yourself. Make sure there is quiet and the judges are looking at you. Then explode into the kata. Don't rush through the movements though. Focus and lock in your muscles on each and every technique; then pause a moment before the next technique to highlight what you have just done. Every time you move, your head should be a split second ahead of the rest of your body. It should snap into place, however, with the same degree of emphasis that you put into your punches and kicks. It is, after all, as much a part of the kata as the striking techniques. (Remembering all the minor details, like this one, creates the impression in the referees' eyes that you have done *all* your homework and you will feel better for it.)

When you move, move with your hips. Make sure they carry your body around the ring, not your feet. They should carry your body into every technique—especially the body shifts. Transitions must be smooth and quickly and quietly done, but not hurried. Remember: Your hips are your center of gravity, your gyroscope. Correct hip movement will keep your body aligned and balanced and your techniques will be fluid and powerful.

Another thing you can do to make your kata stronger is to tighten your fists. It enables you to punch a little bit stronger because you're focusing and locking in your forearm muscles that much more. Your punching techniques will appear a little more clear and crisp to the referees and you will get a higher score if only for making it easier for the referees to see and consequently score your kata.

The referees will also be looking at your posture and stance. Is your stance correct? Is it deep enough? Do you stay in it through the entire kata? Is your spine straight? The spine holds up your body and it is the base of all your power. The same idea applies in weight-lifting, for instance. If you're leaning forward for too long a time after you pick up a weight, you'll either slip a disk or even crack your spine. If you are leaning forward or back in karate when doing a technique, you can't deliver as much power as you should because your body is not aligned and your technique is going to come from a shaky base. Consequently, your technique is going to be bad.

Good karate technique means that both your feet are planted on the floor, that your posture is correct, and that you have speed, balance, finesse, and snap in your punches and kicks. Referees expect to see all these ingredients and if they're missing, your score suffers. They don't care how hard you move or punch. They're looking for good karate technique. Just to show power is no big deal; the judges know that you don't need karate to put power in your punch.

Something else a great many kata performers forget to do is kiya on those moves that call for it. They believe kiyaing is just not that important. They are dead wrong. It *is* important. It's part of the kata, not window dressing or a gimmick that you can just throw away. And don't be embarrassed about kiyaing (yelling). It was put into the kata for a purpose. It tightens and focuses your stomach and chest muscles and enables you to put extra power in your punches and kicks.

There are those people who believe they are so talented that they can throw away the preceding advice. Instead they will tell you that they have their own special style that they apply to kata, that they put their personal seal, their imprint, on their katas. But if you watch them closely, you will also see that too much personality damages both the kata and the self. The performance is no longer of a prescribed kata but rather of a quasi-creation that the judges cannot mark. And if the kata is transformed into something it isn't, then it is no longer effective as a teaching aid. It cannot teach you the moves and blocks and punches correctly. The kata is classic in form and is not to be tampered with beyond a certain—and small—point.

The last few moves and the bowing out are other areas that are often overlooked in training by many karatekas. They end up rushing through them and have points deducted from their score without their realizing why. Or I'll sometimes see a karateka ruin a beautifully executed kata by breaking into a smile just as he finishes and bows out of the ring. To repeat what I said earlier: The last moves you make are the ones the referees will remember, so make them strong. Kiya on the last move and sharply bring yourself to attention with a smart snap. Now is the time to keep your poise. Don't let your body sag or heave a sigh of relief. You *never* show emotion in that ring—in kata or sparring. No one should ever know what you are thinking or feeling. Your face should just be a stone mask because your kata is on display, not you. And remember that your performance is over only after you have bowed out of the ring. So if you are feeling elated or depressed, keep it to yourself, even when your score is announced.

After you come to attention, face the head referee and bow to him. Wait for him to return your bow, *then* bow out and step out of the ring. Etiquette in competition is always noticed. It's that extra little something that sometimes carries the day.

Warning. If the unmentionable does occur and you happen to make a mistake, don't hesitate—continue and finish the kata as though you hadn't done anything wrong at all. Who knows, you may not have. And if you indeed have, the referees may still not have caught your error. If you hesitate, however, it will only make any error that much more obvious and the referees will deduct from your score that much more.

But no matter what horror you think you've committed in the ring, *do not stop*. Ever. If you do, you're out of the kata competition in that tournament. You cannot go back and start all over again. You have one shot. There are no second chances.

After you have performed in a number of tournaments and get to know who your top competitors are, you will then be able to gauge how you will place in competition against certain people, barring any mishap, to within one or two places. You will see a particular kata opponent in a tournament and know exactly which kata of yours you need to perform in order to win, for by then you will know all of his strengths and weaknesses.

Likewise, as you get to know the judges, you will learn how to perform certain katas in certain ways. If you see traditional karate masters refereeing your kata, for instance, who "know" their karate, then you will perform a strong, traditional kata without deviation from the form. Top kata champions know that you have to adapt if you want to win.

CHAPTER SEVEN

Sparring in Tournament Competition

FIGHTING STYLE

Sparring is the end toward which you have been working ever since you began training in karate and sparring in tournament competition will be the closest you'll ever get to actual street fighting—the noise, the pressure, the intensity of your opponents, and the crowds all combine to proximate the conditions that appear in a street fight. The action similarly will be short and conclusive. The difference between the two situations lies in your intent: You are *not* trying to maim or kill your opponent in the ring but effectively use karate techniques to score points and hone your fighting skills.

Yet even those karatekas who understand this vital distinction often fall prey to using picturesque techniques in order to dazzle the judges and their opponents. They are often influenced by the great number of movies, television programs, and magazines that constantly showcase this type of karate strategy to the exclusion of everything else.

Sport karate, however, is *not* a series of spectacular techniques for a very simple reason: They leave most karatekas who try them in incredibly vulnerable positions. When I was eighteen and very cocky about my abilities, for example, I decided to impress my opponent in a tournament with a spinning back kick, only to get punched in the back of my head as I spun around to deliver the kick. Like that alert karateka, I doubt whether

your opponent will stand still to watch you spin around to deliver a kick to his body. This applies not only to spinning back kicks. Attempting to score with round kicks or hook kicks always leaves your groin area wide open to assault and you could incur severe injuries.

I have had over twenty years of martial arts experience and I think one of the best ways to spar in the ring or fight on the street is to use a variety of techniques derived from the bread-and-butter basics. I emphasize this because it's your ability to consistently use the basics with imagination and skill that will enable you to win with a much greater degree of success and with a minimum number of injuries. Besides the possibility of getting seriously hurt, the odds of actually hitting and affecting your opponent with a fancy high kick to the head are not that good. Not only is the head a small target—it is also very hard. Instead, you should go for the body, an area larger, softer, and infinitely more capable of sustaining more injuries.

With all these basics, you ask, where is the element of surprise that allows you that vital split second to paralyze your opponent's defenses and score? If you think that can only happen with dazzling techniques you are very wrong.

Karate, rigid instructors to the contrary, enables you to use techniques in a variety of ways. For instance: To get a tall, strong, and fast man to drop his guard, you need only kick at his stomach with your left foot, wait till he blanches or drops his hands to protect himself, and then drive home a reverse punch to his gut or solar plexus. Another way to open up your opponent's defenses is to charge him, throw your shoulder out as if you're going to deliver a blow, abruptly freeze, and then, as his defenses have let down when he sees that you're not going to attack, shoot out a strong backfist.

As you can see, complex, high-risk techniques are not necessary. There *are* alternatives to those dazzling yet dangerous moves that seem to take a great many karatekas' fancies.

There are other things to take into consideration when you train for and spar in tournament competition. Among them are knowing the rules of the tournament in which you are competing, dealing with and using "psych" techniques, knowing and displaying ring etiquette, developing poise and self-control, and being able to cold-bloodedly size up a situation, plan your strategy, and then execute it successfully.

GETTING HIT

The purpose of sparring in tournament competition is *not* to see who can throw more punches or who can take more punches—who will destroy whom first. Rather, it is to see how effectively you can hit. Can you pick your spots, cross distance, work your technique?

When you're training, are you learning how to do all that—in spite of the pain you will probably have to go through. Regarding training and fighting through pain: My advice to those karatekas who want to compete but are still afraid of getting hit (and hurt) is that people who are afraid of getting hit *will* get hit. Don't even caution yourself about "protecting" your weak side because people always get hit in precisely those places where they are most afraid of getting hit. If you stick to using good techniques, you can minimize

your injuries; but in order to learn anything in karate, you must accept the fact that everyone, not only you, must endure a certain amount of pain. The very nature of karate demands it since it is a contact sport.

There is another way that you can minimize the risk of injuries besides consistently using sharp, clean techniques: by not hesitating *as* you're about to deliver your techniques.

If you hesitate in a match just as you are about to throw out a kick, for example, you will telegraph your intentions to your opponent without knowing it. Now, if your opponent is as inexperienced a fighter as you are, then both of you will kick together and damage each other's legs. On the other hand, if he's an experienced man, he'll either wait for you to kick, step back, and punch you after you've finished kicking the air or he'll jam your leg as it's coming up and then punch you in the chest. Even if he does neither, he'll always be prepared for the kick. He'll always know when you're going to throw it.

Another point to remember about getting hit: In training, as in competition, don't ever fight *against* your opponent—fight *with* him. Otherwise, as I keep on saying, you're going to get hurt. The best fighters instinctively blend into their opponent's pattern of fighting; consequently, both fighters learn from each other and rarely get seriously hurt.

USING TOURNAMENT RULES

Knowing the rules of the various local, regional, and national tournaments is especially important. If you don't, you can be hurt in the standings—and quite often physically as well.

Let's say you know that one particular competitor likes to hit to the face with a jab or backfist and relies on similar techniques to win his matches. If the tournament's rules say no contact to the face, you can be pretty sure that your opponent will be an easy win since he won't be able to do any of his bread-and-butter techniques. On the other hand, if you make the mistake of thinking that a particular tournament doesn't allow hitting to the face when in fact it does, the consequences can mean a broken nose, jaw, or a split and bloodied face.

Don't always expect your opponents to be on their best behavior, however. In a match, whenever you see your opponent breaking the rules and trying to hurt you by punching and kicking to your face or groin, you can exercise one of the following options: You can say to the referee "This kind of match is not for me" and bow out, which is not so good; or you can give your opponent measure for measure. (Of course, successful blocks are best for avoiding injuries.)

There are more subtle points to consider than knowing whether or not a tournament's rules and regulations allow hitting to the face. For example: If the tournament prohibits facial contact, does it still allow techniques that come close to the face to be awarded points? If it does, it means that you can still use your backfist in the match.

This is where poise and self-control come in. Instead of going to the face for blood, you go for points—if you have the muscle control that will allow you to do that. If you don't, and keep hitting the face, then all you're doing is scoring points against yourself.

As you can see, the more you know, the more you can plan. Ask yourself, for instance, what is considered a valid target area for this tournament. By knowing that, you can devise strategy without worry.

If the back is a legitimate area to hit, your opponent probably won't turn his back to you, because if he does, he knows that he will get scored on immediately. If a tournament doesn't allow hitting to the back, then you know that your opponent might come in and punch and then turn around and run away—which is not, by the way, a very good way to train in karate. If you use that type of strategy, you may win a match or two but you will eventually pay the price on the street.

No matter what the rules of the particular tournament are, however, don't ever drop your guard. Always stay alert in the ring and never give your opponent the least chance of tagging you. You never drop your hands when the referee says *yame*—stop—for instance, because your opponent may not hear it and break your nose. Or he may indeed hear the referee and break your nose anyway. Just stop whatever action you're doing, keeping your defenses up at the same time, and go back to the line.

A minor detail that can become very major in certain tournaments is kiyaing when you throw your techniques. Many times not kiyaing enough is overlooked by the referees if you deliver good, strong blows to a valid target area of your opponent. But kiya anyway so the following won't ever happen to you. In 1968, when I won the U.S. International Karate Championships, I had to hit my opponents four, five, six times with clean shots before being given a point by the referees. I couldn't understand why it was happening but Tom LaPuppet, who was coaching me then, picked it up immediately.

He saw that only those competitors who kiyaed when delivering a punch or kick were being awarded points. And I wasn't kiyaing at all. So whenever I finished a match LaPuppet would say, "You've got to open your mouth; you've got to kiya." But I was so intent on beating my opponents that I forgot about kiyaing. Luckily, I woke up in time and said to myself, "Oh yeah, kiya." From then on, I kiyaed and immediately scored.

PSYCH TECHNIQUES

Now that you're aware of how important tournament rules can be on the outcome of a match—or a championship—you should also know about another neglected area of strategy. This takes place outside the ring for the most part but, nonetheless, it still has an incredible amount of influence on the outcome of a match. I'm talking about psych games and the kind of people who play them in order to defeat their opponents before they even step inside the ring.

First off, you should know that in any major tournament, there will usually be 500 or more people competing from various regions of the country and everyone is going to be jockeying for position and for prestige and for recognition. You can easily become a little wide-eyed, not only at the number of people there, but also at the "name" fighters or champions who will be competing with you in the tournament.

When I first began competing I would walk into a tournament with my friends from my dojo and we would only talk to each other since we didn't know anyone else. As we looked around we noticed people oohing and aahing at certain individuals as they moved about with their cliques: "Oh, wow, there's Bill Wallace, there is Chuck Norris, there is this guy, there is that guy."

As *I* started winning national tournaments and getting written up in the magazines, my face became known in the martial arts community. Soon I became accustomed and aware of the fact that as I was walking about, people were looking at me and talking about me. If you're smart, it's something that you use to your own advantage.

But in the very beginning, before you're able to make a name for yourself, you're just a nobody to everyone but yourself. Yet you still want to project a professional image in order to intimidate the people who are going into the ring with you.

My friends and I used to work with what we had—ourselves. We would make sure, for example, that we were always visible as a group. So instead of slouching into the hall one by one we would go marching in together, in numbers—in strength.

Once, two of my dojo brothers and I walked into a tournament wearing the same type of outfit but in different colors. I wore a pair of blue slacks, a blue crewneck sweater, and a white double-breasted blazer, with a blue kerchief in its pocket. One of the others had the same outfit but in pink; the third had the same in lavender. For that particular tournament we also had our gis dry-cleaned and kept them on the hangers. We wanted to look superclean, sharp. We didn't even dress into our gis for a while; we just held onto our hangers with the cellophane still on them. We were showing everyone that we were ready—that we were professionals. That forced everyone to take notice of us and in the process we gained a psychological advantage over our competition before the tournament even began.

As we competed in more and more tournaments, we became more proficient at shaking the competition. We often varied our approach or image for a particular tournament to throw our opponents off balance. At another tournament, for instance, we didn't wear well-cut ensembles but walked in with dirty sneakers, dirty jeans, and sweatshirts that were cut down at the sleeves—rough-and-ready get-up. We were hoods that day. At the next tournament our gis were underneath our arms and our belts were hanging down around our necks. We were sweaty and smelly. Our body language also wasn't refined—we were slinking through the crowd passing the message that if you wanted to mess with us you were crazy—because we'd kill you.

So keep in mind that everything you do in a competition is important, not merely the moment when you finally step into the ring. There *are* other things to consider: to whom you talk, how you walk around, and what you do. (Remember, however, that these are tactics that worked for me at that time. You will have to use your own imagination to find suitable ways to express yourself.)

At times, I would loosen up in the ring; at other times I would go onto a bench and fall asleep—before my matches or between matches. I did this to show my lack of concern.

There were also techniques I learned by watching other, more experienced competitors. For instance, after a while I saw some karatekas wear towels around their necks. And the fact that they remembered to bring a towel and that they had tape in their bag and a first-aid kit impressed everyone greatly. That they had everything that they needed or could want at their disposal meant that they were professionals—they knew what they were doing. And some people envied that. Including me. Some people felt they couldn't, or shouldn't, wear a towel around their neck because people would say: Who the hell are you? Some superstar or something? So they were afraid to do anything at all—even though they could have if they had a mind to. But they were afraid of what other people thought of them so they didn't and missed out on the advantage of doing such "crazy" stunts.

I used to walk out of the dressing room with a towel around my neck, put it down on the floor by a ring, step on it, and wipe my feet—making sure the ring was clean. I was showing other people that I simply had to have certain things done before I would compete. Then, when I finished, I picked up the towel, wiped my feet again, looking very satisfied, and walked away.

I didn't stop there, however. Even after I had easily won a match, I was still setting up the next match and my next opponent. I would constantly be looking around and thinking, hanging around after a match I had just won minutes before. I would say out loud to no one in particular, "No, something didn't feel right in this match," knowing full well that I had just obliterated my opponent. "Nah," I'd continue, "I was a little bit rusty. I'm going to get it together for the next match." Things like that, said within earshot of everyone, contribute to psyching out your opponents and you should continuously work on it throughout your competition.

Remember that there are always psych games going on so make sure that you don't become a victim of one yourself. Look to and learn from the other fighters with more experience. Practice some of the things you feel might suit you and try them out in competition. The more you practice them, the more accomplished you will become. You will soon reach the point where no one will notice the fact that you are playing mind games on them. Competitors who do look at the more

seasoned veterans and learn from them are the ones who benefit most in the long run. If you don't, you're foolish. You're only hurting yourself—you're shutting out knowledge and experience.

Don't let all this talk fool you into thinking that your competitors stop trying to psych you when you step into the ring. A lot of what happens inside is also done purely for psychological reasons. Some instructors might call them fighting tactics but call them what you will, you will be well-served to learn them.

If, for example, your opponent is lying on the ground after slipping or getting knocked down by one of your techniques, don't attack him. Simply back up to the line, stand straight, and wait for him to get up. Why not press your adantage? For two reasons. One, he has the better position anyway, since you would be forced to leave yourself wide open while going down to him to deliver a technique. Two, by backing off, you're saying to the referee and to your opponent that you don't *need* to attack him when he's down—you're strong enough to fight him head on. It also shows everyone there that you're in control of yourself, that you have discipline.

Here's another instance where backing away can be of help in the sparring ring. Once you've effectively used a technique, move back. Now make your opponent come to you; force him to cross the distance to you. What you have done is to reverse the rules of the game: Normally, he who advances is considered the aggressor. In this case, you're manipulating your opponent into coming to you but you're letting him know it, so you have the edge instead.

Another example is how you react to getting hit by your opponent. If you happen to get hit in the solar plexus, let's say, and your body reflexively doubles over, it would be a normal reaction. But if you grimace and walk around before going back to the line to resume the match, you will have signaled to the referee and to your opponent that you're hurt and your opponent will now try to pressure you even more—now that he knows you're in a weak position. To repeat what I said in the previous chapter: Don't ever let your emotions show in that ring, whether you're in pain or ecstatic about executing a superb technique. Never give yourself away. You can, of course, play possum and fake injuries to one side in order to bait your opponent into attacking you there but don't take the risk—he may not see your "bait" or he may ignore it.

Then there is your conduct after *you* hit your opponent. If, by accident, you hit your man very hard, don't stop the action and apologize. Say you're sorry *after* the match. If you say it during the match, your opponent might think that you're really sorry and that he doesn't have to worry about being hit any more. He'll beat you then because he won't be afraid of you any longer.

There is also a reason why you *should* intentionally hit hard. (Not to the face or groin, necessarily, but to a legitimate part of the body.) To illustrate what I mean, I'll recount an incident that took place during the early '70s when I was fighting on the national tournament circuit.

In 1973 I fought an eighteen or nineteen-year-old karateka who was in superb shape. I wasn't, however, in great condition since I was in semiretirement and was teaching in my dojo rather than training for competition. As a result, I knew I had to gain an immediate advantage if I wanted to win the match. When the match started he came in with a kick that I blocked. I then countered and hit him with a punch to the body that dropped him. When he got up I was in my stance, letting him know with a deadpan "look" that there was more where that came from. For the rest of the match his nerve failed and his techniques didn't have the spark that they should have had. Why? Because in the back of his mind he remembered that first hard punch and it acted as a deterrent for the remainder of our bout.

This is, I suppose, as good a place as any to spend some time talking about the "look" I gave my young opponent and why it is a good idea to cultivate one to intimidate your oppo-

nent, and let him know that you mean business. The stares and glares that professional boxers use in the ring before and during their matches are not for the benefit of the magazine photographers and television cameramen. They do it to intimidate and cow their opponents. While it may not work every time, it does work on those souls who have been softened up.

Another excellent psych technique that I have often used successfully in the ring is to fake a punch or kick and get a reaction, then back off from my opponent, shake my head up and down and say "Alright," as if to say, "Aha, *now* I know you," and then come in again with a technique that I carry through on. Once he's unsettled, thinking about himself and what error he's committed, he's already defeated because he's unbalanced enough so that he's lost his concentration and his mind is elsewhere.

FIGHTING TACTICS

Before you step inside the ring, make sure you're loose—not just physically, in your joints, but mentally as well. The reason for this is simple. The tighter you are, the more upset you are likely to get and the less you're going to see—what your opponent is doing and what you're doing. Consequently, you're going to get hit.

Before your name is called, get all the kinks out of your system. And once you step inside the ring, don't just stand there waiting for the referee to start the match. Watch your opponent and don't stop until you have both bowed to each other and walked out of the ring.

The more you look at your opponent, the more you are going to learn about him and the less you're going to be surprised. You're going to learn what techniques he likes to use and when he likes to use them, when and where he's hurt, how he stands up under pressure, whether he relies on a coach too heavily.

But the first thing to look at when he takes his first step at the start of the match is his stance and posture. Is he in a front stance, side stance, or back stance? Each one has distinct advantages and disadvantages that can help you during the course of a match.

If your opponent is standing in a side stance, for example, you know that he's going to be throwing techniques from the side that's facing you; his other side is going to be useless to him and you won't have to worry about getting hit from that angle. Now that you know he is going to be flicking out side techniques—side kicks, hook kicks, round kicks, and back-fists—you are going to have to modify your strategy accordingly to counter them.

In addition to your favorite techniques, you might consider two that I have used to great effect in dozens of matches over the years. While they are more dangerous to use, they are also very effective in helping you out of tight spots. The two techniques I'm talking about are jamming and countering, and sweeping—and the variations that you can work on those moves.

Against some opponents, for example, you will find it necessary to jam someone's leg or arm and counter with a punch or kick if you are to score at all. An extreme example of this occurred when my dojo fought American Karate pioneer Peter Urban's dojo in the late '60s.

Mr. Urban's students all fought in a cat stance, where there is little weight on the front leg. It's more or less free so it automatically kicked out or was raised every time someone from our dojo tried to advance and come in with a technique. However, Mr. Urban's students lost the majority of their matches with us because our dojo members *knew* what they were going to do whenever we advanced, so we simply rushed in, jammed their legs with our own, and then punched them in the chest to score.

Jamming, however, is tricky in that you must know exactly what technique your opponent is going to throw and then be able to time your jam perfectly to catch your opponent before he actually delivers it but *after* he has committed himself. If you try to rush in and jam his leg and he's shooting out a back-

fist, you're in very big trouble. And if you come in either too soon or too late on a punch or kick, you either leave yourself wide open for a counter or get hit immediately by missing the leg or arm.

Since sweeping can be dangerous if you don't know how to execute the technique, a quick review of the mechanics of sweeping will help to keep you from injuring yourself unnecessarily. First of all, you seldom sweep your man from the inside (from inside his front leg) for two reasons. One, that will only buckle his front leg, not sweep him off his feet; and two, you will probably injure yourself in the process since you will be hitting bone against bone (against his shin). When you sweep with your back leg from the outside, however, you're hitting the meat of his leg, his calf. By the way, you always hit, or sweep, the leg with the arch of your foot.

Sweeping, however, can also be very dangerous to you if you don't know when to apply it and to whom to apply it. The very first thing you should do is register the type and kind of stance your opponent is in and his posture.

Is it a front stance, a back stance, or a side stance? When you've done that, look to see whether it is a good, strong front stance, with the weight on the front leg, or whether it's a weak stance, with the weight evenly divided on both legs. If it's a shallow stance, where the weight is evenly divided, then you have a better chance of sweeping. If it's a deep stance, on the other hand, with the knee over the big toe and the weight on the front leg, then he'll be difficult to sweep. (But if he's standing too high up he will be an easy target because of his high center of gravity.)

Second, look at and evaluate the person himself. If he's big and strong then you're going to have a hard time sweeping him off his feet because of his weight and strength (especially if you're short and slight). The same consideration, however, goes for short, squat people, whose low center of gravity makes them more powerfully balanced than they actually seem to be. (Don't try the sweep, however, if you're tall and have to maneuver to get at his leg, becoming unbalanced yourself and the target for a counter sweep.) But if your opponent is tall and thin, it will be much easier for you to take out his leg, no matter whether you're short or tall yourself.

The next thing you should do is test your opponent's reactions against the sweep to see whether he will stay and fight or run and hide. Fake or feint a sweep or kick with your hip and leg and notice how he reacts against it. (Rotate your hip quickly as if you're about to bring your leg around to kick or sweep.) Do *not* tap him with your leg, using a "soft" sweep to test his balance. You'll only be signaling him that you have sweeping on your mind. In addition, many tournaments now have rules forbidding the use of such traps, regarding them as not full, legal kicks. On the other hand, if you just shake your hip and leg, he won't know whether you are coming in with a kick or a sweep. Now check out what he does.

If he uses a reverse punch, you know that he's a puncher—instead of a runner or a blocker. Now you know what you have to do to successfully sweep your man: Jam his hand and then sweep with your leg. If his reaction is slow, however, you don't have to jam at all—just sweep. But if he steps back quickly, you're going to have a problem trying to sweep a man who is going to be running away every time you move in to him, especially as you have to be close to him if you want to execute a sweep correctly. You then have to draw him in toward you using various stratagems which I will go into a little later on. In any case, don't ever run wildly after your opponent for you will just open yourself up for a counter sweep—or worse.

Sweeping is fine and effective as a defensive technique against overly aggressive opponents who try to run you into the ground, since, if you are successful, you have your man right where you want him—on his behind, where he can do no harm to you at all. But sweeping is not always counted as a point in tournaments and while a successful sweep can work for you

in the long run psychologically, it's always good to have that point if you can get it. As a result, try to get into the habit of sweeping *and* hitting, following up the sweep with a punch as your opponent is falling. When you hit your man as he's going down, you do twice the damage you normally would because his muscles are extremely loose at precisely that moment—he's reaching for the ground to break his fall so his muscles cannot be taut and provide a defense against any blows. That way you get your point and do extra damage to your opponent.

Don't be misled by the preceding paragraphs, however, into believing that you are as defenseless as your opponent when it comes to the sweep. Your opponent, like you, has two defenses against the sweep: the reverse punch and lifting the leg out of the way— which takes a lot of experience and excellent timing. For that technique to work, you have to know how to read your opponent and then be able to time the move perfectly.

Reverse punching your opponent, though, even while you're off your feet and beginning to fall down from the sweep, will, more often than not, get awarded the point rather than the sweep, which is not usually considered a valid technique in many tournaments. (You should check, though, to make sure, by asking your instructor or, better yet, a referee at the tournament itself.) I've used a reverse punch myself to score in just this way. I've also seen competitions where a superbly conditioned athlete, victim of a front-leg sweep, recovered as he was falling down to spin around to deliver a back kick into his attacker's chest for the point.

Against any opponent, though, you never do any successful technique more than two times in a row because then you're signaling to your opponent your intentions. He will most probably spot the technique the third time you try it because he will then know where that technique is coming from and how you set up for it. He will then be able to anticipate it and counter effectively what was once a bread-and-butter technique. In addition, when you keep on doing the same technique over and over, you're telling your opponent that he's stupid, which will give you a very angry opponent. What you do instead is mix up that particular technique with other moves. (This is why you never rely on one technique to carry you through a match or competition—a smart karateka will turn the tables on you and you won't be able to score at all.)

The only way you won't fall into the trap of depending on one or two techniques and the only way you can improve yourself as a competitor is by trying out new techniques—experimenting. You'll lose, of course, but that's the only way you will ever learn anything anywhere—in sports, business, or school. You don't learn anything from winning since all winning ever does is confirm what you already know and believe. Never think about winning or losing when you compete—think only of improving your technique. That way you'll better yourself as a karateka, in both technique and etiquette.

But in some instances, sweeping may be impossible and you will have to revert to the jam and counter. If he is in a side stance, for example, it will be harder than usual to sneak up on your opponent since it's very easy to advance or retreat with speed in that stance. You nullify this advantage by jamming his front hand down with your lead hand, leaving his body defenseless, then moving in to punch him in his chest.

You will have to jettison jamming and sweeping altogether, though, if your opponent defends against such techniques by constantly moving around the ring, making sure he stays away from you except when he's coming in to attack, and then beating a hasty retreat.

ADDITIONAL FIGHTING TACTICS

To counter a runner's constant motion strategy, make sure *you* control the action in the ring. Take charge by getting in close to your man and then moving him around the ring in a circle in a clockwise direction. Don't let him dictate how the action will take place. Step to your left and he will follow by stepping to your right so that you won't get a step on him. You will soon have some momentum going so that every time you move, he will make a countermove. You gain your advantage by slowly inching up each time you make a move to your left. When you take your time and gain on your man by increments, you insure the success of your sweep that much more since the key is not to let your opponent know that you're moving up on him or that you're moving him around at will—that he's being used. After doing this four or five times, you should have decreased the length of your step so that you can move in, get around his front leg, and sweep and punch.

There are other things to watch for at the beginning of a match and throughout the match as well. You can gain an important edge over your opponent if you see that your man can fight only with his left foot forward to your left foot forward or his right to your right. Why? Because then he can't work either side of the body comfortably. To take advantage of his "incapacity," body shift, changing your lead foot, and force him to follow your lead. You're now one step ahead of him and will remain so as long as you initiate the action. When that happens, you've won the match. Now, when he follows your body shift with his own, he's left himself wide open for a second, so take advantage of the opportunity and hit him with a punch or kick to score.

Body shifting—and then kicking—during a match can also be the element of surprise that I talked about in the beginning of the chapter, especially when you haven't body shifted once up to that point. Even if your opponent has quick reflexes, chances are he won't be able to block a kick coming in toward his punching, rather than his blocking, side.

There are several other cardinal points of strategy that, when used well, will help you through a great many matches. They vary from considering how to use the clock to your own advantage to knowing what defense to use against various styles of karate.

1. When in doubt, throw out a punch.
2. When someone's charging, reverse punch him.
3. If you have to move, don't just step backward. There are two other directions you can step to—your right and your left. You can more likely evade an onrushing opponent by stepping sideways since you can never outrun anyone by going backward. But if you find that you can only retreat by stepping back, then keep throwing punches out as you do so, forcing your attacker to perhaps get hit in return and break off his attack.
4. When you fight against Korean stylists (tang soo do, tae kwon do) who will be throwing round kicks to the sides of your body and kicks to your head, raise your hands to both sides of your head to block them and protect yourself and then counterattack by immediately rushing in with punches.
5. Don't lose track of the time. (Matches generally consist of one 2-minute round.) If you're behind in a match (down by points) there's no reason why you should stand still. If you wait out the clock, you will just lose. If you constantly attack, however, you have a 50/50 chance of winning. Force the action. Cut down the ring so that your opponent will have to run to either side of you in order to escape. That's when a punch or kick should meet him. If he doesn't react that way, don't be discouraged. You can also run him out of bounds: In many tournaments, if you do it three times during a match, you're awarded a point.

However, if your opponent is behind on points, don't attack—he'll come to you. Wait until he does and, just as he's about to move in—not when he's there, but just as he's moving—step in with a punch.

WATCHING THE STARS

I'm going to finish this section by talking about the problems young competitors face when they start copying the modified techniques of the older and more experienced champions they see in competition. I used to imitate the name fighters when I first broke into competition but after using the techniques that they displayed, I discovered that they are nearly always harmful and not beneficial in the least.

The champions I used to see, for instance, would leave their hands open until just before impact, when they would suddenly close up their fingers into fists. They would also place their thumb to the side of the fist rather than on top of the first two fingers. It made them look, they hoped, a little more flashy to the crowds and their opponents. That positioning of the thumb, however, while it may seem to have more style, is the weaker one to use—you can't get as much power from it because the fist simply isn't being kept as tight as it should, and, consequently, the forearm muscles aren't being totally locked in.

Unfortunately, a lot of champions turn to style for its own sake and abandon their basic karate—not intentionally, I think, but through their pursuit of style they erode their technique to the point where they become ineffective karatekas.

Whether it is the champions of the '60s or '70s, the pattern is always the same. People want to put their personal signature on their technique, so they add some flair to every move until their technique no longer resembles karate—and, indeed, is no longer capable of being karate.

Basic karate may not be very flashy, but it works—if you use it.

CHAPTER EIGHT

The Development of Sport Karate

Sport karate began its life in tournament competition in the late '50s and early '60s on a small scale with sport karateka radically changing the "art" as they adapted techniques to the sports arena that were originally meant to maim and kill. In self-defense karate you try to incapacitate an opponent with one blow; in sport karate you have to fight an opponent in a match that lasts two, three, or even four minutes. Concepts had to change and the way techniques were done also had to change. For those reasons the great names of the '60s set the standard for succeeding generations for they influenced both competition and teaching philosophies with the new techniques and tactics they introduced into tournaments. That is why they are legitimately called pioneers and respected for the role they played in what is considered the classic era of karate.

We can begin with Chuck Norris, a man who has become the spokesman for karate based on his tournament record in the '60s and his more recent movie career.

Norris was an exemplary champion in that he was both a tough fighter and a true gentleman. As a result, he was always looked up to by the public and his fellow competitors for his sportsmanship and skill. To me and to many other teenagers just coming into our own in the mid-'60s, Norris was also an inspiration.

As I went to more and more tournaments, I noticed that he came to each and every one always ready to smile and sign autographs. He was never too tired, never too busy to give of himself and he was always courteous. He was fully aware that he set an example for a lot of the younger people and felt the responsibility of his position. But what was unusual about him was that he always lived up to it and never disappointed his fans or the public.

In the ring, he was a very clean fighter and everyone knew that he would never take any advantage over an opponent other than what sportsmanship allowed. He exemplified the idea "Don't get mad, get even." When he lost a match (a rare occurrence), he didn't talk about how the referees had cheated him out of the championship—even if they had. If he was wronged, he simply chalked it up to experience. His answer was to go back into training for months of hard work, come back on a return match, and totally vindicate himself by beating his opponent.

His philosophy was that if he lost, the fault was his, not the referee's. He never blamed anyone for what he did or did not do in a match since he always felt responsible for his actions inside the ring. As a result, he never complained and he never bad-mouthed anybody—to their face, behind their back, or any other way. (Even though it was typical of those days to do just that—knock someone else down verbally so that you could advance over his back.) Everybody was working to develop a reputation and jockeying for position in the martial arts world. Norris, however, kept to himself and if he didn't do as well as he thought he should have on a particular day, seemed to feel, "Well, I guess I just wasn't sharp today. I'll have to train a little bit harder." And he would go back and train harder. And the next time he won.

While he was Middleweight Champion of the World through the mid- to late '60s, he won every major title worth having in the United States. And the tournaments he won were not exclusively of any one style. He captured East Coast and West Coast tournaments, Chinese tournaments, Korean tournaments, Japanese tournaments, and open tournaments. All of these he won several years running.

His martial arts pedigree in itself is fascinating. While he initially trained in moo doo kwan tang soo do, a Korean style of karate, he rounded out his martial arts education by continuing his training in shotokan karate, a major Japanese style. Norris evidently did that to improve his chances in competition by learning how to improve his muscle control and knowledge of hand techniques, which moo doo kwan does not emphasize. He studied shotokan long enough to effect a total change in his fighting system and ended up fighting from a stance that was a mixture of both Korean and Japanese styles. In fact, what it was was a precursor of what you could call, for want of a better name, American karate—adapting techniques from every style to develop an effective and practical fighting system. As a result, you couldn't really pinpoint Norris as being exclusively a Japanese or Korean stylist.

When I became a black belt in 1968, Norris was already a legend in karate circles so we all were watching him very closely in the tournaments. After following him for a while, we began to pick up on his unique style of fighting.

Norris fought from a back stance, which was typical of the Koreans in the '60s, but which he modified because of his Japanese background. He distributed his weight evenly on both feet, rather than standing in either a full back or front stance. He also used to keep his hands in tight fists with both arms out in front of him—similar to the John L. Sullivan boxing pose.

Throughout his career, one of his most favored techniques was the spinning back kick. I soon realized that before he did this kick, his lead hand, the left hand, would begin to open up and his fingers would start playing back and forth to distract his opponent. His arm would then begin to go up and down and his fingers would follow suit by also moving up and down. Then, all of a sudden, he would spin and throw the back kick. (That's the kind of detailed observation that can help you beat even the best opponents.)

The man who complemented Chuck Norris' career—in that he was Norris' nemesis—was Joe Lewis, a country boy from North Carolina. Their relationship was similar to the Joe Frazier/Muhammed Ali rivalry: two great champions came along at the same time with different fighting styles. Each one brought out the best in the other during the course of their matches and made them extraordinary events to see. It was to the great benefit of sport karate, especially to the people who trained in that era and were in their formative years, that top champions were there to show everyone how good karate could be.

Both men's fighting careers began around 1965 and ended around 1970. The two of them were exact opposites both in fighting style and in personal temperament.

Lewis did occasionally beat Norris but it was Norris who came out on top at the end of their careers with a decisive edge in the number of matches won. The reasons for this were simple. Norris had a general arsenal of well-developed techniques that he used in all of his matches. He didn't just rely upon several types of kicks or hand strikes. And when Norris did lose, he found fault only with himself, thinking something was lacking in his own development. For him, the only way to change that was by training harder and by learning new ideas. Besides all that it was Norris' extraordinary perseverance and superb sense of timing, and the combination of his great heart and natural abilities that made him an almost unbeatable foe. Joe Lewis, on the other hand, was a totally different character. His favorite techniques were lightning-quick side thrust kicks, backfist strikes, and reverse punches. These three techniques invariably destroyed his opponents and he won most of his matches by relying on those moves.

While both men had big followings, their fans attached themselves to their respective fighters for totally different reasons. Norris' came to cheer him on to victory, while Lewis' went because they wanted to see him lose. While Norris was likable, Lewis was arrogant. That didn't detract from him as an athlete for Lewis was a formidable champion—a heavyweight, with the speed of a lightweight.

A good example of Lewis' athletic prowess is the fact that he earned his black belt in under a year's time. When he went to the Japanese island of Okinawa to study karate, he was considered one of the best *natural* fighters ever to have trained there. His instructor was obviously impressed with his abilities because he promoted Lewis to black belt after only nine months of training.

Lewis was not tall and thin; he had a massively built six-foot, 200-pound natural athletic body. To his credit, he was smart enough to exploit his extraordinary physique by always wearing a gi that was about three sizes too small. As a result, it didn't quite fit around his torso and his huge chest muscles were always very prominent. The sleeves on his jacket would just barely come down to his elbows so that his massive forearms would also be constantly exposed, along with his outsized knuckles and fists.

The impact that this made on opponents was just devastating. When you stepped into the ring for your match and faced the man, you *knew* you didn't want to get hit by him, to get caught by any of his techniques, because you instinctively felt that if Lewis connected you were in for a very painful experience.

During his career, Lewis was already teaching his own brand of karate, primarily tips on tournament fighting, which he called "the inverted angular attack." I would call it a de-

layed reaction attack: Throw out your shoulder, forcing your opponent to react, and a split second later, when his defenses are just beginning to relax, throw out the backfist.

Of course, the reaction he got from this tactic and the one nearly everyone else got were two different things entirely. When this overpowering man began to move toward you and then throw out his shoulder, your hands *immediately* came up to protect your face. But then, instinctively, as he abruptly stopped, you realized that he wasn't going to follow through, so you began to relax—and then got caught with the backfist.

Also unlike Norris, Lewis was much more reserved toward his fans and resented the intrusion that autograph seekers made upon his time and privacy, His attitude was that he didn't come to sign autographs; he came to fight. He carried that attitude with him everywhere he went and he never seemed relaxed before any of his matches. At a tournament, he would remove himself from everyone, sit by himself in a corner, and remain there to concentrate on his strategy for the evening ahead.

But when he stepped into the ring, he was all action. Lewis was not a gentleman. He kept hammering at you until he beat you. Lewis had to win; Lewis had to persevere; and he had to destroy his opponents—and he did. Whether it was in bare-knuckle competition, where he built up an unbelievable record of wins, or in full-contact karate boxing, where he was Heavyweight Champion of the World for a great many years, Lewis was the one man with whom nearly everyone was a bit hesitant to step into the ring.

Two stories can illustrate just how awesome Lewis' speed and power were and also show what type of character he had. In 1969 a tournament called "The Orient versus America" was held in New York City to put to rest the controversy of who was more talented: the Oriental or the American.

In the tournament, Lewis was seeded to fight against someone named Tanaka, who was a very small but powerfully built Japanese who looked as though he would be more at home in judo, where he held a much higher belt than he did in karate. Lewis towered over Tanaka by over a foot; standing next to Lewis, Tanaka came up to Lewis' stomach. The weight difference was 200 pounds to 130 pounds in Lewis' favor.

The time came for them to begin their match and they bowed to each other. Lewis immediately got down in his side stance, skipped forward, and began to shoot out his powerful side thrust kicks. Tanaka was trying to pick up on the timing but in the meantime he was catching the side kicks on his shoulders despite his speed and agility. Each time one of Lewis' kicks hit him, Tanaka went flying out of the ring. Even though there were no ropes around the boundaries of the ring, he was literally kicked out of it. His feet left the ground and his body was blown back, just as if there were a rope tied around his waist and it was violently being jerked back. To the people in the stands it was unbelievable, because with every kick that Lewis threw, Tanaka kept flying back.

But Tanaka, great technician that he was, began picking up on Lewis' timing after getting kicked out of bounds a number of times. The next time Lewis shot out the side thrust kick, Tanaka shifted to Lewis' inside, ducking underneath the side kick, and grabbed hold of Lewis' gi. Tanaka then executed a judo throw, taking Lewis over his shoulder and dumping him on his back.

After a moment's delayed reaction, the audience were brought to their feet, their mouths gaping. Lewis, however, was probably more surprised than anyone else because in one instant he was throwing out his fast side kicks and in the next he was looking up from the floor. But aside from admiring the mastery of the throw, it couldn't be awarded a point—it wasn't a karate technique. However, the crowd now began to cheer for Tanaka to win the match.

Tanaka had now obviously figured out how to counter Lewis' side thrust kick but Lewis' ego or pride wouldn't permit him to change

tactics midway through a match. As a result, Tanaka continued to body shift to Lewis' inside on his side kicks rather than running back in retreat and trying to evade them. The match progressed and the side kicks kept coming; Tanaka kept shifting inside and kept delivering solid reverse punches to Lewis' wide open chest for points.

Since Tanaka was able to score more often in this manner than Lewis did with his strategy, Tanaka was awarded the decision. But Lewis refused to leave the arena, upset that the judges had given the bout to Tanaka after he had knocked Tanaka out of the ring so many times. He pointed out to the judges that Tanaka didn't hurt him in the least. How could they give him the decision?

This, however, was one of the few times that Lewis lost and his reputation grew to the point where promoters were soon only looking for people who they were sure had a good chance of either destroying Lewis personally or his legend.

One such contest that has stuck in many people's minds was a full-contact bout that Lewis fought in Sunnyside Gardens, Queens, against Ronny Barcoot of the Carolinas, who was also an Okinawan stylist and just as powerfully built as Lewis.

This took place in the early '70s, when full-contact karate boxing was becoming popular, and the crowd which came was more or less divided into two groups: those who felt that Lewis would destroy Barcoot and those who felt that Barcoot would be the first one to beat Lewis in full-contact boxing—because he was just as strong, just as quick, and a superb karate man as well.

The old animosity toward Lewis still remained, however, since Lewis was constantly giving interviews saying that nobody could touch him and that he was the best in karate. So a great many people came, as before, just to see *him* get beaten up. But no matter how you rooted, you always bought tickets to a tournament if Lewis was in it. He had that kind of presence.

The match began and they kicked around a

bit to take each other's measure. Barcoot kicked Lewis in the stomach several times and Lewis shook his head up and down to acknowledge the fact that, alright, Barcoot did have a little power. Then, about a minute or so into the first round, Lewis' attitude suddenly changed. Whereas for the last minute he was feeling out his opponent to see exactly what he had in power and technique, Lewis now dropped down into a crouch, into his side stance, planted his feet firmly into the canvas, and as Barcoot came in to attack, hit him with a left jab that knocked Barcoot out cold for several minutes.

Sitting ringside, I could see that when Barcoot got hit in the face with that jab, his body hung in the air three feet above the canvas, actually straightening out level with the ground for a few seconds before finally falling down. The power of that short jab was just terrific. While Barcoot was indeed a good, strong fighter, he became just another victim of Lewis' overwhelming power.

That match was a good indicator of the impact that Lewis made as a champion since quite a lot of people who saw him fight were encouraged to train to try to become as great a champion as he was. Norris and Lewis, though in different ways, were pioneers that subsequent karateka emulated. In this respect, they both drew a great many adherents to the martial arts.

There were other fighters who didn't become as well known as Norris or Lewis but who still made a sizable contribution to the martial arts during the time they spent in tournament competition in the '60s.

One such man was Hawk Frazier, who fought in the late '60s. It is a measure of his ability that people who were around then still remember him with tremendous respect. Like me, Frazier came out of George Cofield's shotokan dojo in Brooklyn. His uncanny ability and love for throwing perfect flying kicks quickly earned him the fear and respect of all who faced him—as well as the nickname "Hawk." In the ring it wasn't a question of his beating you and winning the match, it was more a question of whether or not you would *survive* the match.

When Frazier was a brown belt, for example, there were black belts who came into the dojo in Brooklyn and challenged our instructor and his top students to free-for-alls. Frazier would invariably fight them and just as invariably leave them on the floor.

After one such fight, a second-degree black belt with tears in his eyes and blood pouring out of his mouth ended up pulling off his black belt and throwing it in the garbage. He did that to indicate the extent of his humiliation and also to show everyone there that he realized the wastebasket was exactly where his black belt deserved to be.

Physically, Frazier was a marvel. All 175 pounds of his six-foot one-inch frame was solid muscle. He looked like a fine, thoroughbred racehorse, with not an ounce of fat on him. He was one of those rare natural fighters who, if he chose, could have gone into boxing and easily become a world champion.

A personal story can help to illustrate just how devastating Frazier's power was. We were once sparring in the dojo, he at half speed and with half the power he was capable of, and he hit me in the chest with the heel of a spinning back kick. On impact, I felt what I would expect to feel if I had been hit point-blank by a bazooka instead of the heel of someone's foot. I thought my breast bone had been shattered. I couldn't even take my gi off; I couldn't even move my arms. All I could do was just stand and try to breathe.

Holding my arms down to my sides, I unfastened the ties on my jacket by moving just my wrists and hands. After someone removed my belt I let my body lean to the left and the gi opened up one way. Then I leaned my body the other way and the gi jacket fell off. I still couldn't move my arms so someone had to dress me. When I got home, I immediately lay down in order to breathe normally—but not very deeply. I was hurting for weeks before I could use my arms, much less take deep breaths.

Just imagine the injuries Frazier's opponents received in the ring in tournament competition. After all, he hit me with just half of his power. Quite simply, he obliterated everyone he faced. Unfortunately, his career only lasted a few years and ended in 1970—some say because of his actions at the end of the International Convention of Martial Artists in December 1969, the forerunner of the WUKO World Championships. While it brought together the top champions from Japan, Europe, the United States, Canada, and South America for competition, its main goal was to provide an opportunity for top karateka to reach a consensus so that a world body could professionally shape the growth of sport karate in the years to come.

The tournament itself featured such champions as Dominic Valera of France, who was French and European Champion several years running, and Toyotaro Miyazaki, who was then All-Japan Champion.

Miyazaki was eliminated during the preliminaries, leaving Valera, Frazier, myself, and an East Coast fighter named Fowler in the finals. I lost to Frazier and Fowler lost to Valera. Fowler and I then fought a match for third place, which he won. Now Valera and Frazier faced each other for the championship, which included a diamond-studded belt.

Valera was far more experienced than Frazier, who was all of twenty years old, but to many people, not a stronger or better fighter. Frazier's great asset was his genius to adapt and to instinctively learn techniques in literally a matter of seconds.

For example, some years earlier, Bob Shapoff, one of the dojo fraternity, left the dojo for the Army. Since he was stationed in California, he went down to Los Angeles to train with Mr. Nishiama, who was by then a legendary karate instructor. He trained with Nishiama for three years, his tour of Army duty, and then returned to the dojo in Brooklyn.

One of the first things he did was to spar with Frazier, probably to try out what he had learned in California and to see how good he had become. Two of the things that Mr.

Nishiama's students were very good at were posture and foot sweeps, so it was expected that Shapoff would try to sweep Frazier.

To everyone's surprise, Bob Shapoff took no stance, which was very unconventional to us, since we were always taught to fight from a very rigid and low front stance. He was standing straight up and as Frazier attacked with a lightning fast technique, Shapoff very easily and without any concern body-shifted and swept Frazier's leg out. The next thing we knew Frazier was sprawled out on the floor.

They were sparring again a minute later except that Frazier now did the exact same foot sweep and it was Shapoff who was on his rear. What stunned everyone was that Frazier had never even seen the technique before. He felt it only as he was being taken out, yet he immediately knew how to work it to perfection without having to practice it even once. This extraordinary physical intuition—understanding a technique after seeing or experiencing it just one time and being able to repeat it thirty seconds later in the same match—was what made him a world class athlete and an awesome opponent.

Valera, however, like Joe Lewis, had extraordinary speed coupled with great size and strength, not to mention years of experience in the international arena. At that time, Valera also had a powerful technique that was impossible to defend against: He took the front leg out with a strong foot sweep and followed it with a lunge punch. That technique is not unusual now but in those days it was practically unheard of. To compound the problem, when you finally did see it, it took months before you were able to figure out a counterattack or just effectively withstand it. The reason for that was that everyone was still relatively isolated in the '60s. So if somebody developed a technique that you hadn't seen, then hit you with it, you wouldn't know how to deal with it for quite some time. It took time for you to first overcome the newness and then it took some more time to take it apart to see what made it work. Finally you had to spend time and effort on figuring out an effective block and counter.

To deal with Valera's sweep-and-punch was doubly frustrating, however, for along with its newness was Valera's expertise in working the technique. He had refined the combination to such an extent that he scored the great majority of his points with it and it became a staple in his repertoire of techniques.

Valera, who was called The Big Cat because of his great size and speed, started the match by doing just that. He took Frazier's front leg out, came in as Frazier was falling, and drove in a lunge punch. He immediately got the point. A couple of seconds later Valera came in with the exact same technique and again swept out Frazier's front leg, but as Frazier was falling, he spun around with a back kick and planted it squarely in Valera's chest. Frazier, in fact, almost knocked him out. It was a superbly executed counter-technique that earned Frazier his point and the match continued on in that fashion. In the end, Valera scored a controversial point and won the match and the championship. But the people in the stands booed the decision.

Frazier, who was a very headstrong and very intense young man, then asked for the microphone. It was not an unusual move since it was customary in those days when being presented with a trophy, especially in our dojo, to publicly thank our teacher for his work and to give homage to our instructor by dedicating the trophy to him.

Perhaps everyone expected Frazier to do just that but when he took the microphone, he said to the audience instead, "You know as well as I do that I beat him and that I was cheated."

This short speech so upset both the audience and the magazine reporters that Frazier's career took an overnight plunge. He picked up a bad reputation just for that one line and he paid the ultimate price—his fighting career was ruined.

Tom LaPuppet, on the other hand, was a different man entirely. To say that he was one of the great champions and gentlemen of the sport during the mid- to late-'60s will sound like hyperbole, unless one considers that he was the second karateka to be inducted into the Black Belt Hall of Fame in 1969, after Chuck Norris in 1968, and the very first black man. Just for a black man to be given that kind of recognition in karate, or in anything else during the '60s, is a testimonial to both his character and his ability for he was one of the most colorful champions and among the greatest technicians to ever grace the sport.

His karate was so formidable that he could show you a dozen variations on such a basic combination as an overhead block and punch. LaPuppet's real name, as a matter of fact, was Tom Caroll. He was given the name La-Puppet by his peers as a tribute to his originality and his ability to continually invent new techniques. This vaunted originality was the result of traveling toward his goal in a route never thought of before by previous karateka and was chosen for him partially because of the way dojos were run in the United States over fifteen years ago.

In the '60s, dojos were recognized as being exclusively one style, whether it was tae kwon do, shorinryu, or shotokan, and there was a parent organization one had to belong to if one wanted to advance beyond the basic black belt level. If anyone left the parent organization, as our dojo did over political matters, then all dojos were closed to him.

As a result, the only way to learn new techniques was to "steal" them by watching other fighters or instructors do something in public, memorizing it, and reconstructing it later on in the privacy of your own dojo. When La-Puppet would see a top fighter, for instance, he would return to the dojo and imitate his movements, and as he tried to mimic the way the other fighter had moved, he began to understand why that karateka's shoulder was in that particular position, or why his stance was deep, and what benefits or drawbacks each part of a person's fighting strategy had to offer him. Through imitation, he analyzed the other fighter's strengths and weaknesses, understood his capability, and consequently learned how to beat him. It was quite an effective method for him. During the four years he competed, from 1964 to 1968, he won most of his matches.

One technique that LaPuppet brought into tournament competition was the front *thrust* kick. He took the front snap kick, modified it by thrusting the kicking leg straight out and used his hips to get that much more reach and power out of the kick. Its success was due to several things. First, it was difficult to execute. You had to thrust your hips all the way out in order to do it correctly, which meant that the momentum carried you forward onto the balls of your supporting foot, making it an extremely delicate maneuver. Two, it was difficult to effectively block because it was easy to misjudge its striking distance and defenders usually blocked what they thought would be a short snap kick. The technique's deceptiveness turned it into one of LaPuppet's bread-and-butter techniques. He successfully used it to defeat such a stellar champion as Bill "Superfoot" Wallace (World Middleweight Champion for most of the 1970s)—an accomplishment few men have ever repeated.

When LaPuppet walked into a ring, he always shook hands with his opponent and bowed courteously, whether the man he was fighting had thirteen years of experience or three months of experience. His attitude was unchanging. When he won the match, he went over to his opponent and he shook hands with him and congratulated him on a strong fight. When he lost a match, he also went over to his opponent and congratulated the man on a strong fight. He had the same rule for everyone: If that man was facing him in the ring, he gave that man respect as an opponent. And just like Norris, no one ever heard LaPuppet say, "I was cheated." This despite the fact that LaPuppet definitely *was* cheated a number of times, not only because of style prejudices, but also because of racial prejudices.

For example, he won a tournament one year by virtue of beating everyone there was to beat and they could do nothing about it. The next year he was defending champion, which meant he didn't have to fight in the eliminations at all; he only had to fight against the winner of the preliminaries. But rather than suffer him to just fight one match in the finals, the tournament directors changed the name of the tournament slightly and then told him that he was no longer the defending champion. He, then, naturally had to fight in all the matches. Everything else in the tournament, however, was the same as before—the site was the same, the rules were the same, and the people who were running it were the same.

LaPuppet had to face such as this all the time yet I never heard him complain about anyone's prejudices or shortcomings or stupidities. He accepted what happened, although deep down I'm sure he knew what was going on and decided that the way to fight it was to beat them. Not to whine or get mad, but simply to get even. This was typical of LaPuppet's character. "You want to cheat me? OK. I can't argue with that. But if I beat you so decisively that I beat not only my opponent but those who want to deny me what's mine by right, then you'll all have to give me my due out of respect for my abilities because they're so superior to yours. Whether you like it or not, you have to give me my respect."

After he retired from competition, he coached me as I fought in tournaments across the country and I learned from him over the years to become more of a gentleman. But LaPuppet never criticized me when I acted in an impetuous manner. His philosophy was that everyone makes his own bed and lies in it. He taught by example rather than by telling you what he thought you should do. The more matches I fought and the more I traveled with LaPuppet, the more I learned to step out of the ring with a smile on my face, whether I won or I lost.

CHAPTER NINE

Refereeing

One of the most important areas in sports is that of judging competition. Consequently, one of the most talked-about and problem-filled areas in all tournaments is the subject of fair and impartial refereeing.

In karate this problem is especially troublesome because the sport itself is so young. Sport competition followed upon the introduction of karate to this country after World War II by about fifteen years, so the inability of the sport to organize itself responsibly, especially in an area as sensitive and subjective as refereeing, is understandable. Nevertheless, no one has chosen to face the problem that exists in this area and that is specifically preventing karate from advancing itself and making itself known to a much greater number of people than it presently attracts.

In most tournaments the directors call together on the morning of the competition all the black belts present, whether they're competing in the tournament or not, and they quickly explain to them a set of rules almost entirely different from the black belts' last tournament. This will be the set of rules for that day's competition. It is discussed, some points are clarified, and the black belts are then encouraged to go out and do a very good job of refereeing.

The problems with this are manifold. To begin with, you're not quite sure in many tournaments whether the people who are judging are actually even black belts since the people running the tournaments usually don't ask for any proof of their karate background.

But even if they have an extensive karate background and know how to throw the various kicks, punches, and blocks on a legitimate black belt level, that doesn't necessarily mean that they have ever competed in a tournament. And even if they have competed in tournaments, *that* doesn't insure that they have any idea how to referee or that they have had prior refereeing or judging experience. At any particular event, therefore, you may not have good judging or refereeing—despite the good intentions of the black belts running the matches.

After refereeing in local, regional, national, and international tournaments for over ten years, I have found that most karatekas fail to see the essential point that just as teaching karate requires you to learn skills separate from those of acquiring a black belt, so does refereeing. It is a separate area that needs special attention and individual training. The fact that a black belt has mastered all the kicking and punching techniques of his style in no way indicates that he is a good referee or even that he has had referee training.

This seemingly simple problem persists in most tournaments, however. In addition, the people who *are* refereeing far too often don't have a good or deep background in the martial arts and as a result usually don't—*can't*—have high and durable criteria with which to judge a match. In the end, the most common fault is that a referee will give the match to someone who is of the same style as he is. A person trained in shotokan or tae kwan do or issinryu or any other system of karate tends to be biased in favor of people of his own style for two reasons.

One is that he likes to have his "own" people win, whether they are friends of his or not and whether they are members of his particular club or dojo or not.

The second reason, however, is usually what influences someone's refereeing more often than any other factor. Understand that it is not that the average referee is cheating. He isn't. The average referee is interested in giving an adequate and fair score but he is prejudiced—whether he realizes it or not—by the very fact of his having studied in a particular system. He feels that only the techniques and katas in his style are done the correct way, whereas the techniques and katas in every other style have areas that have not been perfected or that simply leave something to be desired as far as style goes. As a result, he is going to be prejudiced, without realizing it, against other karate systems simply because he has been led to believe that the way he practices karate is the *only* way to practice karate.

This has presented the majority of tournaments with the continuing problem of having unqualified judges officiate and score matches. The only answer is the most obvious one—to train referees. The best solution would be to have one association specifically charged with the training and certification of arbitrators, referees, and corner judges—similar, for instance, to the setup that exists in boxing.

Unlike karate, boxers aren't permitted to judge competition. Instead, their association professionally trains and certifies referees and judges and assigns them to officiate at all boxing matches. These referees in fact need not have ever practiced boxing; they may not have ever put on a boxing glove. But they have been trained in the one set of official rules and, allowing for slight rule modifications in different states, they have been legally certified by the athletic commission of their particular state as people who can officially interpret the association's rules.

The only organization that has done just that on a worldwide basis is the World Union of Karate Organizations, which has been accepted as a governing body for sport karate by over seventy-five countries. Representatives from these countries sat down to draw up a viable plan of refereeing and judging and arrived at a consensus as to what group of rules and bylaws would not only govern competition on an international level but also that would be codified by a refereeing council representative of its members.

Members of the council are chosen to represent the different continents of the world—six men representing the six continents. While not everybody is satisfied with all of the laws, which is understandable and normal, WUKO is flexible enough in its outlook to allow for changes to be made when a majority demands them. So if an individual coach or competitor can convince his representative to persuade the other members of the council that his particular rule change is to the karate community's benefit, then you will have a new rule. If he can't convince them, then the rule is not adopted.

For every country that is a member of WUKO there is an organization that represents that nation's karate committee and that has adopted WUKO's rules for tournament competition. In the United States that organization is the Amateur Athletic Union, since the AAU has adopted the WUKO rules for competition in AAU sponsored tournaments. The effect of this is to slowly create a truly uniform set of regulations for competitions around the world.

The AAU runs clinics around the United States in order to train people in the AAU/WUKO rules of competition. People interested in becoming officials go to the clinics and have the rules explained to them by AAU members who are nationally and internationally rated referees—who have had extensive experience working the rules in the ring and can instruct people in the intent of the rules. Besides explaining the rules and regulations, the AAU also teaches prospective referees how to use their hands to indicate exactly what type of blow was scored and how it was scored; corner judges are taught how to use a set of flags to signal their responses to the action that takes place in the ring.

AAU referees begin their "uniformity" by wearing a specific uniform to all AAU sponsored tournaments, whether it is in California, Kentucky, or New York. Their slacks are grey, their shirts white, their ties red. This immediately sets AAU officials apart from everyone else so that on entering a hall you instantly know who is a referee and who is a competitor. It not only dresses up an event but, more importantly, clearly gives the officials a recognizable position of authority at the competition.

The core of the AAU program is not that it issues licenses but that it has codified the different standards in refereeing in a number of levels.

Level E certifies individuals only to chart and keep score of matches. The AAU has a specific method which is the same from one AAU tournament to the next.

Level D signifies a greater capability in charting and allows the individual to begin corner judging in local level AAU competition. AAU rules specifically state that level D officials start gathering judging experience at the smaller local level in order to get practical experience along with those competitors who are also just breaking into tournament competition.

Each corner judge has an official judging book that he brings to every tournament and has signed to certify that he indeed did judge a certain amount of matches at such and such a place on such a date. After he participates in a number of tournaments and feels he is ready to advance to the next level, he takes a written test that accompanies every promotion. If he passes the written test and the follow-up evaluation by a higher level official, he is then promoted to level C.

Level C upgrades the individual by letting him corner judge at state level tournaments and sometimes in regional tournaments. In addition, he will be refereeing from time to time at local level AAU events. Thus he slowly upgrades his experience in different areas of refereeing and judging. After taking another written test and being evaluated once more, he can become a B level official, which allows him to be a corner judge at all regional and some national level competition and lets him referee at all local and most state tournaments.

After a period of time, he can become a level A official, which entitles him to be an arbitrator, referee, and corner judge at all national and international competition. The position of arbitrator is the key to running trouble-free tournaments and should not be discounted as a fancy but essentially insignificant job.

Every match has six officials assigned to the ring—one arbitrator, one referee, and four corner judges. The arbitrator sits directly behind where the referee is standing, oversees the activity in the ring, and handles all protests, which can only be made by a competitor's coach. (The competitor lists his coach on his tournament application and only that individual is allowed to coach him during a match, where he sits or stands along the boundary of the ring.) If the competitor and/or coach sees a violation of the rules, then the coach directs that protest to the arbitrator. The arbitrator then does one of three things. He explains the referees' and judges' decision, calls upon the referee and judges to explain how they arrived at that particular decision, or lets the referee and judges know that a rule has indeed been violated and overturns their decision. I'll illustrate this with an example.

One of the most neglected areas of competition is penalizing those competitors who constantly run out of bounds. At every tournament, the director mentions that anyone caught running out of bounds and avoiding the fight should be penalized. However, in practice this admonition is rarely enforced during the competition. The AAU rules strictly on the matter, however, and it is rigidly enforced. It allows a competitor to go out of bounds twice without being penalized. He is merely given an official warning. The third time he goes out of bounds, whether he runs or was forced out (barring, of course, if he was hit, flew in the air, and then landed out), the referee officially tells him—for the third time—that he was out of bounds *and* automatically awards one point to his opponent.

Let's say competitor A runs out of bounds three times but the referee either forgets the rule or neglects to keep an accurate count of how many times competitor A stepped out of bounds. He therefore forgets to award competitor B his one point and allows the match to continue. At this point competitor B's coach lodges a protest with the arbitrator that competitor A had stepped out of bounds three times yet wasn't penalized. The arbitrator then mentions to the referee that he must penalize competitor A and award competitor B one point—which the referee then does.

These types of cut-and-dried violations of the rules are what a competitor and his coach can protest about to the arbitrator. The AAU, however, doesn't allow protests to be made that are "judgment" calls, such as when a coach says to the officials, "Why didn't you give my man that point. I thought that punch scored to the midsection of the body perfectly." This is the opinion of the coach as opposed to the opinions of the referees and the judges. Unfortunately for the coach and his competitor, the referees' and judges' opinions are what count. They have been trained to determine which points scored and which ones didn't, which punches were blocked and which ones weren't. The coaches and competitors must take the position that even though they may disagree with the referee's opinion, they should settle back and accept things for what they are. "I certainly disagree with this judgment, but these are the officials and I will stick by their decision." This kind of attitude is the only one that will bring unity to the martial arts and that will benefit everyone. You must remember that one of the reasons that the media do not cover many of the tournaments is because of the major discrepancy among the various competitions in both refereeing and officiating. When karate can

standardize under one umbrella organization all the different rules, it will advance the sport and better the kind and type of publicity it receives. If it can't and continues to have stubborn individual instructors who insist on having their way 100% of the time, then competition will continue to suffer. Karate will continue to have five hundred different rules which are accepted by no one. The result is that competitors will continue to be forced to adjust to a new set of rules at every tournament in which they compete, making it that much more difficult for them to take advantage of their athletic abilities.

For just these reasons, all graduates of the AAU certification program have licenses enabling someone licensed in New York State, for instance, to travel to California, where he might not be known at all, and officiate at an AAU tournament merely by showing his license and referee book to the chief referee. That book and license indicates to the chief referee that he is in fact licensed to referee under the AAU rules and has actually officiated at such tournaments, in such places, at such times. The chief referee now knows how advanced he is in refereeing and how much ring experience he has and can assign him to judge, referee, or arbitrate in the tournament where he will do the most good.

All officials must understand that basing their judgment on anything other than the merit of the techniques only harms the integrity of the sport of karate. Too often, this is due to faulty assignment of personnel. Officials are called upon to judge or referee a match or matches where people from their association or club are competing and this can easily present a conflict of interest for the official(s) involved.

Because of the frequency of this practice, it's important to know how you view the tournament experience itself—what victory and defeat mean to you. On the one hand, each competitor wants to win all his matches all of the time. On the other hand, tournaments can be a testing ground and learning experience, the method by which you achieve your goal of perfecting your karate technique. In that case, when you win a tournament, you know that you have triumphed over your opponents for that day only. And when you lose in a tournament, you know that you need to determine what was the reason or reasons for the loss—what you did wrong, what you didn't do enough of, and what you did too much of. You will then have material to work on for the next competition and so improve your skills.

Officials can help to promote this attitude through impartial and fair refereeing. If we all do that, we upgrade the standards of karate competition and increase its reputation by influencing the competitors to strive to be the best that they possibly can. If we're not as objective as we can be, we do a major disservice to our students. If one of my students is fighting in a match and he's not good enough to beat his opponent, yet I still award him the match as referee, I only reinforce in him a false sense of confidence.

If the competitor is interested in perfecting his technique, he will immediately understand that his instructor is cheating for him. In other words, his instructor doesn't have confidence in his ability to beat his opponent on his own merit.

Of course, you don't find too many students who will stand in a ring and say to their instructor who is refereeing, "Hey, wait a minute, I didn't land that shot." Sometimes a student may not be aware of what's going on and if he is, he usually won't say anything. He will begin to feel, however, that his instructor is either incompetent as a referee or that he's cheating for him. This will ultimately, especially in the eyes of a younger student, make him feel that if his instructor is in the ring refereeing his match, *he* doesn't have to worry—his instructor will always make sure he wins. He will then feel that cheating *can* actually make up for his lack of superior technique and the idea of cheating is thus legitimized in his mind as a valid tool in sport competition. This is contrary to everything we allegedly believe in karate-do and everything that we, as instructors, are supposed to be teaching our students.

Equally as important is the fact that the student, if he is not aware that his technique didn't honestly score, will believe that he *is* good. After all, the match was awarded to him. And when he feels that he is a good karateka and competitor, his interest in progressing and in perfecting his technique will not be as keen because he feels that he has already perfected his technique. He can prove it since he's won so many matches.

Finally and most important, cheating for a competitor for whatever reason gives the referee the feeling of being above the law and ultimately that can only lead to the disintegration of karate as a sport.

All in all, when people scream about cheating in tournaments, they don't realize that most of the time it's not cheating—by and large it's plain incompetence. Not that it makes any difference to the competitor who did a technique well yet didn't have it officially scored. Yet many people immediately assume that when a referee awards a bad decision to someone, it's because of cheating on his part. From the dozens of tournaments I have witnessed, competed in, and refereed, I think that usually it's not a question of bad faith but rather of the referee not being competent.

The AAU/WUKO Handbook printed in the following Appendix clearly explains all the rules and their accompanying admonitions to the referees and judges—what they have to do and how they have to conduct themselves. What makes these rules different and unique are not the rules themselves (though there are rules in the AAU Handbook that are radically different, such as awarding points to kicks and punches that score to the *back* of an opponent). What sets these rules apart and makes AAU tournaments different is that the rules have not only been written down, individuals trained in them, and licenses issued, but that rule books have been printed and made available to all competitors and coaches as well as referees and judges so that someone other than a referee can rectify mistakes in the ring. Since an arbitrator has also been provided, mistakes then *can* be rectified. There is an apparatus that permits negotiations. (For example, going back to out of bounds: Going out of bounds three times entitles your opponent to a point; five times, a second point; six times, your opponent wins the match.)

Appendix 1
Refereeing Terms and Signals and Their Meanings

TERM	MEANING	DEFINITION; DESCRIPTION OF REFEREE'S MOVEMENT
1. SHOBU HAJIME	Start the match	Start of match. The referee stands on prescribed spot
2. ATO SHIBARAKU	A little more time left	A signal will be given 30 seconds before the end of the match
3. YAME	Stop	Interruption or end of match. Contestants and the referee return to their prescribed positions
4. MOTO NO ICHI	Original position	Contestants and the referee must return to their prescribed positions
5. TSUZUKETE	Fight on	Resumption of fighting. Ordered when interruption occurs not called for by the referee
6. TSUZUKETE HAJIME	Resume fighting, begin	The referee, standing in his prescribed position, steps back with one leg and closes his arms, which are widely opened obliquely upward, in a horizontal position in front of his body
7. FUKUSHIN SHUGO	Judges, assemble	The referee calls together the judges, signaling with both arms raised high; the judges assemble in front of the arbitrator
8. HANTEI	Judgment	Standing outside the match area (there is no stipulation as to what specific place outside the match area he should stand) the referee requests the judges by a long-short whistle to express their opinions, and by a short whistle to put down their flags and return to their prescribed positions
9. HIKIWAKE	Draw	The arms are crossed over the chest, then brought down with the palms of hands showing to the front. The arms are held at an approximate 45° angle from the body

10. ENCHO	Extension	Match reopened following the exclamation "Shobu hajime"
11. TORIMASEN	"I don't accept it" (unacceptable as an effective technique)	Technique not accepted as effective; arms crossed before the body are brought down to an approximate 45° angle with the palms of the hands down
12. AI-UCHI	Simultaneously reciprocated blow	No point scored for either party; fists meet in front of chest
13. AKA (SHIRO) NO KACHI	Red (white) wins	One arm raised high in an oblique direction
14. AKA (SHIRO) IPPON	Ippon for red (white)	Scoring technique is indicated, then one arm is pointed downward
15. HANSOKU CHUI MUBOBI CHUI	Cautioning of a foul	The referee points with his index finger to the abdomen of the warnee
16. HANSOKU	Foul, contestant loses the match	The referee points with his index finger to the face of the violating contestant and announces a victory for the other contestant
17. AKA (SHIRO) JOGAI	Outside the match area	The referee points with his index finger to the outer match area and on the side of the offending contestant
18. JOGAI CHUI	Cautioning of stepping out of the match area	The referee points to the spot where the warnee overstrode the boundary of the match area; then to the abdomen of the warnee; and announces an *ippon* for the opponent
19. AKA (SHIRO) HANSOKU, SHIRO (AKA) NO KACHI	Foul by the red (white), victory of the white (red)	The referee with his index finger first points to the face of the violating contestant; then raises his arm above the shoulder toward the winner
20. AKA (SHIRO) KIKEN, SHIRO (AKA) NO KACHI	Renunciation by the red (white), victory by the white (red)	The referee with his index finger points to the position of the renouncing contestant; then raises his arm above the shoulder of the winner
21. SHIKKAKU	Disqualification from the tournament	The referee, with his index finger, points to the face of the disqualified contestant with a loud and distinctive proclamation; then to the area outside the match area; and announces victory for the opponent

22. YAME, JOGAI	Stop, outside the match area	When it has been recognized that there has been an instance of stepping out of the match area, the referee immediately declares "Yame," "Jogai," orders the match interrupted and instructs the contestants to return to their prescribed positions
23. MUBOBI	Foul, when contestant refuses to take up a defensible position against attack	
24. IPPON	Point	
25. WAZA	Technique	

Appendix 2
The Rules of the Match

The following Articles are instituted for the purpose of establishing necessary rules for official tournaments which are to be hosted, organized, and participated in by the World Union of Karatedo Organizations (hereafter to be referred to as WUKO) and its affiliated member countries.

ARTICLE 1: OFFICIALS AND STAFF
1. Tournament chairman and tournament vice-chairman
2. Chief referee and deputy chief referee
3. Referees and judges
4. Chief arbitrator and deputy arbitrator
5. Arbitrators
6. Time keepers, record keepers, procedure assistants, announcers, score keepers
7. Tournament doctor

ARTICLE 2: MATCH AREA
The size of the match area shall be 8 meters square, have a flat surface, and be provided with proper hazard-prevention measures. In the event the match area is to be elevated above the floor, the height shall be one meter and the floor space shall be 11 meters square in principle. The chair for the arbitrator should be placed in this elevated area.

ARTICLE 3: ATTIRE
The official karate attire shall be a plain white karate-gi. The official attire of the referees, judges, and arbitrators shall be decided by the WUKO International Referee Council. (In the AAU, it is grey slacks, white shirt, and red tie.)
Karate-gi must, in principle, meet the following specifications:
1. The jacket, when tightened around the waist with the belt, must be of an even length and cover the hips.
2. The belt must be tied properly as not to impede the match performance.
3. The white and red strings which will be used for a kumite match must be approximately 5 centimeters wide and of a length sufficient to allow 15 centimeters of length to hang from the knot at both ends. They must be distinctly colored, one white and one red, so as to be easily identifiable during a match.
4. Should the referee decide that any contestant's attire may impede a match, he may declare the contestant ineligible to take part in the match.

176

5. The use of bandages or supports for reasons of injury must be approved by the referee.
6. The use of a contestant's identification badge on the front of his jacket or a number on the back must be approved by the Tournament Committee at the start of each match.

ARTICLE 4: JUDGES, REFEREES, AND ARBITRATORS
In a kumite match, the panel shall consist of one referee, four judges, and one arbitrator. In a kata match, the panel shall consist of one referee and either four or six judges. In the case of a match being held lacking the prescribed number of officials, the results of that match shall not be recognized.

ARTICLE 5: TIME KEEPERS, RECORD KEEPERS, PROCEDURE ASSISTANTS, ANNOUNCERS, SCORE KEEPERS
In an official tournament, the prescribed number of time keepers, record keepers, procedure assistants, announcers, and score keepers shall not exceed two in each category for each match.

ARTICLE 6: DUTIES OF TIME KEEPERS, RECORD KEEPERS, PROCEDURE ASSISTANTS, ANNOUNCERS, SCORE KEEPERS
1. The time keeper shall keep time according to notification from the referee.
2. The record keeper shall keep records of the matches according to notification from the referee.
3. The procedure assistant shall expedite the progress of matches according to instructions from the referee.
4. The announcer shall confirm the record of the record keeper in accordance with the instructions of the referee and then announce the outcome of the match.
5. The score keeper shall confirm the record in accordance with the instructions of the referee and put up a notice on the scoreboard.

ARTICLE 7: POSITION OF TIME KEEPER, RECORD KEEPER, PROCEDURE ASSISTANT, ANNOUNCER, SCORE KEEPERS
The time keeper, the record keeper, the procedure assistant, the announcer, and the score keeper shall take their positions behind the arbitrator and they shall be provided with desks, chairs, and any other necessary equipment.

ARTICLE 8: SAFETY DEVICES
The use of safety devices shall be the decision of the Tournament Committee at the time of each tournament.

ARTICLE 9: MEDICAL TREATMENT AREA
The medical treatment area shall be located at an appropriate location adjacent to the match area. At least one doctor must be present at all times who shall be fully equipped with the neccessary instruments, medical supplies, and pharmaceutical products.

ARTICLE 10: PROTESTS

A protest shall not be approved except those made by the registered coach. A protest made after a match has been completed shall not be recognized.

ARTICLE 11: TYPES OF MATCHES

1. Kumite match   (individual, team match)
2. Kata match   (individual, team match)

ARTICLE 12: DURATION OF A MATCH

In principle, the duration of a kumite match shall be two minutes. This time limit also applies to both the first and the second overtimes. However, the Tournament Committee may alter this and further extend the match. The duration of a kata match shall be determined by the type of kata to be performed.

ARTICLE 13: LEGITIMATE AREAS OF ATTACK

1. Head
2. Face
3. Neck
4. Chest
5. Abdomen
6. Back

ARTICLE 14: PROHIBITED AREAS OF ATTACK

If any of the following acts are performed, the contestant shall lose the match by *hansoku*. However, when the violation is slight, the contestant may be given a warning *(hansoku chui)*.

1. Contact to any of the areas mentioned in Article 13.
2. Attacks to the face with the fingers.
3. Attacks to the testicles.
4. Persistent kicking attacks to the shins.
5. Hitting directly with the body.
6. Attacks on the joints.
7. Dangerous sweeps using full arm or body strength.
8. Continuous clinching.
9. Any insulting behavior.
10. Time wasted not concerned with the match.

ARTICLE 15: PROCEDURES

The referee shall indicate the start of the match with the announcement of *shobu hajime* and will announce the end of the match with *yame*.

ARTICLE 16: CRITERIA FOR DECISION

1. Whether an *ippon* has been scored.
2. The degree of fighting spirit and vigor.
3. Whether techniques are superior or inferior.

ARTICLE 17: STANDARD OF *HANSOKU*

Besides the prohibited items mentioned in Article 14 there are two *hansoku:*

1. When a contestant has received three *hansoku chui* during a match.
2. When a contestant has received three *mubobi chui* during a match.

ARTICLE 18: *SHIKKAKU*

Shikkaku shall be decided as follows:

1. When a contestant abandons continuation of the match.
2. When a contestant is prohibited from continuing the match on the order of the appointed tournament doctor.
3. When a contestant protests directly, being dissatisfied with the judges' decision.
4. When a contestant, during the match, disregards the direction of the referee.
5. When a contestant does not appear within the appointed time.
6. In team matches, when the registered order of the contestants is changed at the match area.
7. When a contestant has been given a *jogai chui* three times during a match.
8. When an individual match participant is not able to participate in the match after pairing has been decided.
9. During a kata match, *shikkaku* shall be decided as follows:
   (a) When a contestant stops his performance.
   (b) When a contestant has made an error in the performance of a match.
   (c) When a contestant performs a different kata than announced.

ARTICLE 19: *JOGAI*

Jogai occurs when a contestant steps outside the perimeter of the match area. However, if a contestant falls and lands outside the match area, it shall not be counted as *jogai*.

ARTICLE 20: *MUBOBI*

Mubobi is given when a contestant has no intention of taking up a defensive position for an opponent's attack.

ARTICLE 21: JUDGING STANDARD OF DEFEAT OR VICTORY IN KUMITE MATCHES

1. As soon as a contestant has 3 points (*sanbon*), he is declared the winner.
2. When the match is over and the score is 2 (*nihon*) to 0, the fighter with 2 points is declared the winner.
3. When the match is over and the score is 2 (*nihon*) to 1 (*ippon*), the winner is determined by *hantei*.
4. When the match is over and the score is tied, the winner is determined by *hantei*.
5. When the match is over and the score is 1 to 0, the winner is determined by *hantei*.
6. When *jogai* has been given three times, the offending contestant shall lose a point.

7. When a contestant has lost a point due to three *jogai* previously in the match, an additional point will be lost after two *jogai* and a third point after only one *jogai*.

8. When a *hansoku chui* has been given twice during the match to a contestant, the offending contestant shall lose a point. Furthermore, after another *hansoku chui* is given, the offending contestant shall lose a second point.

9. When a *mubobi chui* has been given twice during the match to a contestant, the offending contestant shall lose a point. Furthermore, after the loss of a point and another *mubobi chui*, the offending contestant shall lose a second point.

10. When a contestant has committed any of the items listed in Article 17 and/or Article 18, he shall be announced as being defeated as *sanbon* will be lost.

ARTICLE 22: STANDARD OF DEFEAT AND VICTORY IN KUMITE TEAM MATCHES

1. In team matches, victory shall be judged by the number of winning contestants. If both teams have an equal number of winning contestants the points of the winning contestants shall be counted. If the total points are equal, a final deciding match will be held. The final deciding match shall be between two chosen representatives of the contending teams. Should the first round prove inconclusive, a second round shall be fought. If at the end of the second round, the match is still inconclusive, the representative contestant of each team shall be replaced by another member of the team.

2. No competitor may participate in more than two consecutive matches. Once withdrawn, a contestant shall not compete again until the entire team has competed.

ARTICLE 23: STANDARD OF DEFEAT AND VICTORY IN KUMITE INDIVIDUAL MATCHES

In kumite individual matches, victory shall be judged in accordance with Article 21. When victory is not decided within the regular match time, an overtime match shall be called. In this case, the first contestant to score an *ippon* shall be determined the winner. If, at the end of the first overtime, no conclusive judgment can still be passed, a second overtime shall be called. This second overtime must, without fail, determine the winner.

ARTICLE 24: STANDARD OF JUDGING KATA

1. The standard of judging kata shall be indicated on the basis of 10 points.

2. Adding each judge's score (excluding the highest and the lowest scores) constitutes the total score.

3. When the total scores of 2 or more contestants are equal, victory shall be determined by the combined scores (including the highest and the lowest).

4. When the combined scores (including the highest and the lowest) are equal, a rematch will be held.

ARTICLE 25: PROTEST

1. No contestant may personally protest against a declared decision.
2. When a decision is considered to be against the Rules of the Match or the Rules of Judging, the registered coach may protest immediately to the arbitrator by raising his hand.
3. For all situations not foreseen in these rules, or in case there is doubt about the applicability of these rules in any given situation, the referee, all judges, the arbitrator, and the chief referee shall consult among themselves to find the solution.

ARTICLE 26: MODIFICATIONS OR ABOLISHMENT OF RULES

Modification and/or abolishment of these rules shall be decided by a majority vote of the WUKO International Referee Council and then be submitted for approval to the Directing Committee.

ARTICLE 27: ADDITIONAL CLAUSE

Regarding anything which is not covered by these Rules, clarifications and interpretations may be made by the tournament body of referees, judges, and arbitrators.

Appendix 3
The Rules of Judging

ARTICLE 1: VOTING PRIVILEGE OF JUDGES
1. In a kumite match, the referee and the judges may exercise the privilege of casting one vote at the time of judgment for the match.
2. In a kata match, the referee and the judges may exercise the privilege of voting 10 points each at the time of judgment for the match.

ARTICLE 2: VOTING PRIVILEGE OF ARBITRATOR
The arbitrator may exercise the right of voting one point only when his opinion is called for by the referee.

ARTICLE 3: DUTIES OF THE CHIEF REFEREE
1. To inspect the referees' and judges' attire.
2. To allocate, reallocate, and supervise referees and judges.
3. Concerning matters not clarified in these rules, the Chief Referee shall make decisions upon consulting the arbitrator.

ARTICLE 4: DUTIES OF THE DEPUTY CHIEF REFEREE
The duties of the deputy chief referee shall be to assist the chief referee and in case of his absence to undertake his duties.

ARTICLE 5: DUTIES OF THE REFEREE
In accordance with the Rules of the Match, the duties of the referee shall be as follows:
1. To give instruction of the rulings to match contestants.
2. To announce the start of the match.
3. To announce discontinuance of the match.
4. To caution contestants violating the Rules of the Match and/or the Rules of Judging or to order offending contestants out of the match area.
5. To call for the tournament doctor to attend the match contestants when necessary.
6. To give instructions for the carrying out of injured contestants.
7. To summon the judges and to dismiss said judges to return to their prescribed position.
8. To announce *hantei* to the judges.
9. To declare the winner of the match.
10. To announce an extension of a match.
11. To announce his vote when the decision of the judges is tied.
12. To announce rejudgment when and if recommended by the arbitrator.
13. To announce the end of the match.

14. To announce the "exchange of bows" at the beginning and at the end of a match.
15. To render a judge's decision "not effective" when only one judge indicates an "effective" attack.
16. To hear the judges' opinion when more than one judge indicates an "effective" attack.
17. To ask the opinion of the arbitrator when it is warranted.
18. To give instructions for the removal of any barriers that may impede performance of a match.
19. To indicate by signal the points in a kata competition.

ARTICLE 6: DUTIES OF THE JUDGES

In accordance with the Rules of the Match, the duties of the judges shall be as follows:
1. In kumite matches—to indicate the decision of the match, according to the referee's direction, by means of a red or white flag.
2. In kumite matches—when a proper attack is recognized, to indicate said attack by means of a flag and/or whistle.
3. In kumite matches—when injury of a contestant, running out of bounds, a contestant falling, or any situation in which the match is unable to be continued is recognized, to indicate said situation by means of a flag and/or whistle.
4. Following the direction of the referee, after a consultation, to give their judgment from in front of the arbitrator's chair.
5. In a kata match—to indicate the points earned by a contestant following the direction of the referee.

ARTICLE 7: DUTIES OF THE CHIEF ARBITRATOR

In compliance with the Rules of the Match, the duties of the chief arbitrator shall be as follows:
1. To supervise the arbitrators participating in each match and to inspect said arbitrator's attire.
2. To allocate, reallocate, and supervise the arbitrators.
3. To investigate protests through the arbitrator in charge.
4. When said protest is recognized as valid, to recommend to the chief referee that a reexamination take place.
5. To make any other recommendations to the chief referee which are deemed necessary to proceed with the match.

ARTICLE 8: DUTIES OF THE DEPUTY CHIEF ARBITRATOR

The duties of the deputy chief arbitrator shall be to assist the chief arbitrator and in the case of his absence to undertake his duties.

ARTICLE 9: DUTIES OF THE ARBITRATOR

In compliance with the Rules of the Match, the duties of the arbitrator shall be as follows:
1. To accept protests.
2. To call for consultation for reexamination.

3. To recommend rejudgment.
4. To supervise the record keepers and time keepers and to inspect and sign the record of the match.
5. To give any recommendation deemed necessary for refereeing and/or judging: in issuing a recommendation, the referee and all the judges shall be summoned through the indication of the referee; to call on all referees and judges through the chief judge for the aforesaid advice.
6. To hear the opinion of the referee.

ARTICLE 10: MANAGEMENT OF A PROTEST

When the arbitrator receives a protest from a registered coach against the judgment of the referee or a judge, it is the duty of the arbitrator to order a break in the match by use of a whistle. The arbitrator then must indicate his judgment for said protest. However, when it is deemed necessary, the arbitrator shall summon the referee and the judges for consultation. If the protest is recognized, the arbitrator shall advise the referee to render another vote. This second decision shall be recognized as effective judgment of the match and any further protest against the second decision shall not be accepted.

Appendix 4
Conducting Kumite and Kata Matches

ARTICLE 1: CONDUCT OF A KUMITE MATCH

1. The arbitrator, record keepers, time keepers, procedure assistants, and score keepers shall take their prescribed positions.
2. The referee and the judges shall take their prescribed positions.
3. Following the referee's instruction, the contestants shall take the prescribed positions and bow to each other.
4. The referee shall announce *shobu hajime* to begin the match.
5. The referee shall announce *yame* when a contestant executes an accurate and effective point.
6. Upon the announcement of *yame* by the referee, the contestants shall stop fighting.
7. The referee shall order the contestants to return to their prescribed starting positions and declare *ippon*, identifying the decisive scoring technique *(waza)*.
8. Immediately following the aforementioned, the referee shall declare *tsuzukete hajime* (continue) and resume the match.
9. When a contestant has executed the third accurate and effective *ippon* the referee shall declare *yame* and order the contestants to return to their prescribed starting positions.
10. Immediately following the procedures stated in 7 above, the referee shall declare the victor, announcing *aka (shiro) no kachi*, by raising his own hand.
11. Immediately following the referee's announcement, the contestants shall bow to one another and leave the match area.
12. When a contestant halts the match without giving any particular reason, the referee shall order the continuation of the match by announcing *tsuzukete*.
13. When a contestant steps out of the match area during a performance the referee shall declare *yame*, *jogai*, and order both of the contestants back to their prescribed starting positions. He will hen announce *aka (shiro) jogai*.
14. When the time keeper signals, indicating "30 seconds left of match time," the referee shall announce *ato shibaraku*. In this case, the match shall continue and not be halted.
15. When the "time-up" signal is given by the time-keeper, the referee shall announce *yame* immediately and order both contestants to return to their prescribed starting positions.
16. Immediately following the aforementioned, the referee shall announce *hantei* and ask for the judgment of the judges. Upon this announcement

all judges shall demonstrate said judgment by raising red and/or white flags.

17. If and when the number of flags raised by the judges is equal, final judgment shall be the opinion of the referee and he shall announce *shiro (aka) no kachi* or *hikiwake*.

18. Judgment of the judges may not be expressed by any means other than by the use of the red and/or white flags.

19. When *hantei* must be given in the second overtime, the judges must indicate red or white only. There must be a winner.

20. When an effective attack is delivered simultaneously with the "time-up" signal, the validity of the attack shall be determined by the referee or after a discussion of the judges.

21. In the cases mentioned below, the referee shall declare *yame*, suspend the match and order the contestants to return to their prescribed starting positions, and resume the match by announcing *tsuzukete hajime* (continue).
    (1) When both contestants are continuously clinching.
    (2) When the attire of the contestants is extremely disheveled.
    (3) When a contestant has fallen.
    (4) When a contestant commits a prohibited attack.
    (5) When it is deemed necessary by any other occasion.

22. The referee shall announce *yame* and temporarily halt the match, order the contestants to return to their prescribed starting positions, and declare, *hansoku chui*, *mubobi chui*, *jogai chui*, or *hansoku* or *shikkaku* in the following cases:

NOTE: These decisions shall be made upon the consultation of the entire panel unless all judges demonstrate their judgments with flags to the same effect.
    (1) When either contestant executes a prohibited attack or indicates the preliminary movement for the said attack.
    (2) When a contestant receives an injury.
    (3) When a contestant becomes sick.
    (4) When a contestant is recommended to discontinue the match by the tournament doctor.
    (5) When a contestant abandons the match.
    (6) When a contestant disregards the referee's cautioning and commits a prohibited attack.
    (7) When a contestant moves outside the match area.
    (8) When a contestant is recognized to be *mubobi* (having no indication of defense).
    (9) When it is found impossible to continue the normal proceeding of the match.

23. Any attack delivered outside the boundary line of the match area shall be invalid.

ARTICLE 2: CONDUCT OF A KATA COMPETITION
The conduct of a kata match shall be as follows:
1. Time keepers, announcers, and procedure assistants shall take their prescribed positions.
2. The referee and the judges shall take their prescribed positions.
3. Following the procedure assistant's instructions, the contestant shall take his prescribed position.
4. The contestant shall bow, standing at his prescribed position, and declare the name of the kata to be performed.
5. Following the referee's whistle, *hajime* shall begin the performance.
6. The contestant shall return to his prescribed position upon completing his kata.
7. Upon the contestant's return to his prescribed starting position, the referee shall signal for the display of scoring by means of a whistle, at which time the referee and judges shall display their scoring.
8. The record keeper shall total each judge's score, excluding the highest and lowest, and give this total to the announcer.
9. Following the record keeper's information, the announcer shall announce the total score.
10. Following the aforementioned announcement, the contestant shall bow and retire.

ARTICLE 3: PRESCRIBED POSITION OF THE REFEREE
The starting position of the referee in a kumite match shall be on the center of the outer edge on the line drawn at a distance of 2 meters away from the center point of the match area. In a kata competition the position of the referee shall be in the center of the outer part of the match area facing toward the record keeper. The referee and judges shall be provided with a chair, scoreboard, and a whistle.

ARTICLE 4: PRESCRIBED POSITION OF THE JUDGES
In a kumite match, the position of the judges shall be at the four corners of the outer boundary of the match area. This position shall be provided with chairs, red and white flags, and whistles. In a kata match, the position of the judges shall be to the right and left of the referee and they shall be provided with chairs and scoreboards.

ARTICLE 5: PRESCRIBED POSITION OF THE ARBITRATORS
The prescribed position of the arbitrator shall be exactly behind the referee's prescribed position and 2 meters outside the match area. The arbitrator shall be provided with a chair.

ARTICLE 6: PRESCRIBED POSITION OF A CONTESTANT
In a kumite match, the prescribed position of the contestants shall be in the center of the outer edges on the two parallel colored lines drawn perpendicular to the front side line, drawn at a distance of 1.5 meters from, and on

both sides of, the center point of the match area. The distance between contestants shall be 3 meters. In a kata competition, the contestants shall face the referee and shall stand at the center point of the match area.

ARTICLE 7: TIMEKEEPING

The time keeper shall be seated behind the arbitrator and shall start the timing of the match with the referee's announcement of *hajime* and stop the timing with the announcement of *yame*. The time keeper shall indicate 30 seconds before "time-up" by use of a buzzer with one short signal and when match time is up, he shall indicate this with two long signals from the buzzer.

Targets and Techniques

	Target of attack	Attack technique
Jodan (upper part of body)	Head, face, neck	Tsuki (thrust), uchi (punch), keri (kick)
Chudan (middle part of body)	Chest, midsection, back	Tsuki (thrust), uchi (punch), keri (kick)

When identifying an effective technique, reference must be made to the part of the body to which the effective attack was delivered. Thus, the effective technique immediately following a "nage" (sweep) must also be described in terms of "jodan" or "chudan."

Order of announcing

Aka (Shiro)	Jodan (Chudan)	Tsuki (Uchi) (Keri)	Ippon

Judges' Scoring with Flags

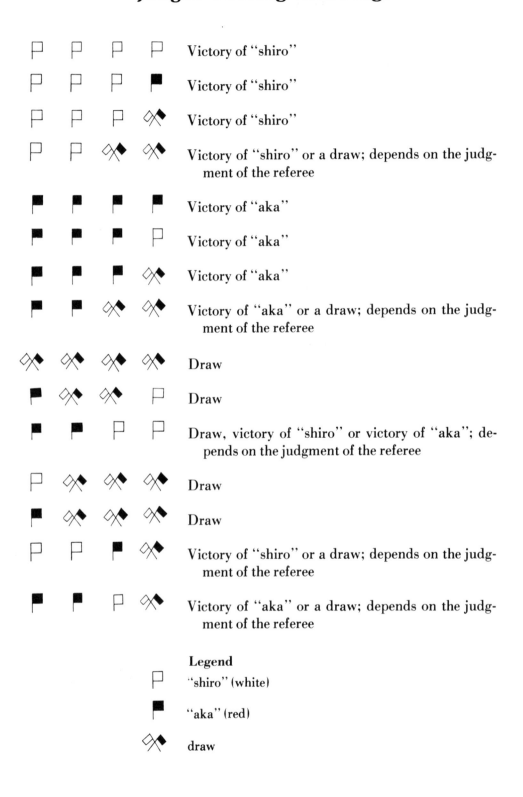

The Match area and the Positioning of the Referee, the Judges, and the Arbitrator

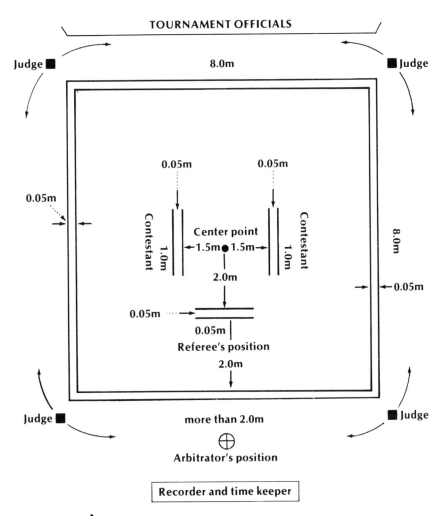

As a general rule, the arbitrator shall be positioned more than 2 meters away from the front side line of the match area. Where technically difficult, however, this rule may be circumvented.

Depending on the floor shape, the recorder and the time keeper may be positioned beside the arbitrator.

As a general rule, all the line markings on the floor shall be in distinct white and 0.05 meter in width.

All measurements shall be made between the outer edges of lines.

As a general rule, each of the judges shall be positioned 0.05 meter away from the corner of the match area. Where technically difficult due to floor shape, etc., this rule may be circumvented.

Index